# GETTING RE... MODEL 3

## ROGER S. PRESSMAN

## Dedication

To my sons, Matt and Mike,
without whom this book would
never have happened

To my granddaughters,
Lily and Maya,
who may never have to learn to drive

# TABLE OF CONTENTS

# PREFACE

The fact that you've opened this book indicates that you have more than a passing interest in the Tesla Model 3—the first battery electric vehicle (BEV) that protects our environment, looks like a high-end sports sedan, offers absolutely awesome tech, is priced at a level that many people can afford, and performs like cars that cost twice as much.

But how much do you really know about BEVs in general and the Tesla Model 3 in particular? If your answer is, "Not much!" then **Getting Ready for Model 3** is a book that just might be worth reading.

**Getting Ready for the Model 3** (GR4M3) is not the definitive guide to Tesla's new automotive offering, scheduled for first deliveries in late 2017. No book can make that claim just yet, because much about the Model 3 is still unknown. But GR4M3 is a worthwhile guide that distills the millions of words written about the vehicle into a cohesive, well-structured whole. It uses information gleaned from forums, blogs, auto magazines, websites, and social media (e.g., tweets from Tesla Motors executives) to produce a discussion of Model 3 that will be of use to every person on the Model 3 reservation list and everyone else who has interest in the car.

GR4M3 allows you to better appreciate Model 3 by examining the exterior and interior of the car; clarifying important issues like range and "range anxiety"; discussing what is known about the car's tech, and explaining charging and autonomous driving, and predicting the cost of ownership. It addresses some of the decisions you'll likely face when you're asked to configure your Model 3. GR4M3 even provides you with a method for estimating when your car will be delivered!

In addition, GR4M3 will give you just enough background to understand some of the very important issues that have a strong bearing on the success of Model 3 and BEVs in general. But do you really need all of this information? I think you do, and here's why. I can guarantee that when you take delivery of your Model 3, you'll get questions. Lots of questions. Some will be from admirers. Some will be from those who are intrigued by Model 3. And, some will be from haters. In each instance, you'll be asked to provide answers, and GR4M3 will help you provide them.

If you've never owned an electric vehicle before, some of the things you learn may seem slightly daunting. Don't let the new jargon, technology, and changes intimidate you. Think about it this way: Perhaps you were initially a bit uneasy ditching DVDs for Netflix—"why can't I just pop in the DVD, it's just so much easier." But once you got used to the seamless user experience and ease of streaming movies, that old DVD technology felt dated… even antiquated.

The same will happen once you take delivery of your Model 3. The learning curve might feel steep early on, but, soon… passing a gas station will surely feel like passing a Blockbuster video store—it will look like a relic from the past.

Throughout the book I'll speculate about certain Model 3 features and options. But I only do this where speculation is sensible and grounded by facts about Model 3. I won't be right all of the time, but by suggesting certain design features and directions, I hope to stimulate your thinking about the car.

I'm one of the relatively few people on the planet who has actually ridden in a Model 3. (I'll tell you about that ride and what it means within the pages of this book.) I was also one of the very first owners of a Tesla Model S and as a consequence, I've had four years of driving experience on the Model 3's older sibling. I'm also an engineer, so I get the techie stuff, but this book isn't for techies, it's for everyone. GR4M3 is written in a non-technical, friendly style with the intent of making you smarter about BEVs and much smarter about Model 3.

**Acknowledgments.** Every book is a joint effort and this one is no exception. It could not have been written without the contributions of thousands of writers, commenters and posters on virtually every conceivable media platform. My sincere thanks to every one of them. And to the many engineers at Tesla Motors—much respect!

My sons and EVANNEX business partners, Mathew and Michael, encouraged me to write GR4M3 and more importantly, contributed greatly to its content by providing a wide array of raw material gleaned from various media sources. Both of my sons (and I) have reservations in for the Model 3. Thanks also go to Nick Howe, author of *Owning Model S*. I've adopted a few of his ideas and more than a little of his enthusiasm as I wrote this book. Many of the excellent Model 3 photos in this book have been used courtesy of our fellow EV enthusiasts Kyle Field and Zach Shahan of CleanTechnica.com | Important Media.

Finally, to my wife Barbara, my love and thanks for tolerating the many, many hours I spent juggling new product development for aftermarket Tesla accessories at EVANNEX, nights writing book # 10 in my home office, and the crazy life of someone who is supposed to be retired.


Roger S. Pressman,
EVANNEX.
Deerfield Beach, Florida


*A postscript:* My sons and I communicate with thousands of Tesla fans and owners worldwide via our weekly newsletter, daily blog, and social media. We do this because breaking news about Tesla occurs regularly, and it's really hard to keep up. To stay up-to-date on the latest news, I recommend that you sign up for our newsletter, check out our blog updates, and follow us on social media. These alternate forms of communication will act as a perfect complement to this book. We humbly invite you into our on-line community at evannex.com.

Mike, Matt and Roger of EVANNEX

# ABOUT THE AUTHOR

Roger Pressman is Founder and Director of Product Development for EVANNEX—the world's leading aftermarket accessories company for Tesla Model S, Tesla Model X and soon, Tesla Model 3. He is also one of the first 200 Tesla Model S owners worldwide. Roger also owns a Tesla Model X and has pre-ordered the Model 3.

During his long technical career. Roger has worked as a software engineer, a manager, a professor, a consultant and an author of ten books. He is Founder of Electric Vehicle University (EVU) and Editor/ Publisher of Nick Howe's popular book, *Owning Model S: The Definitive Guide to Buying and Owning the Tesla Model S.*

Roger S. Pressman

Roger's journey into the automotive aftermarket accessories world began when he ordered the Model S in 2011. During the long wait until the car was delivered, he was concerned that Model S did not have a center console. So he designed and built the now-famous EVANNEX *Center Console Insert* (CCI) in his garage, posting his progress on the forums.

His idea generated substantial interest and support from the Tesla community, and a tiny startup, EVANNEX, was created to provide the CCI to owners who liked the idea. Today, Roger has partnered with his sons, Matt and Mike, and EVANNEX has grown to offer over 50 unique aftermarket Tesla accessories for Model S and Model X, many of which are manufactured in the company's facilities in Deerfield Beach, Florida.

You can learn more about Roger and his aftermarket Tesla accessories company at EVANNEX.COM

# CHAPTER 1
## GETTING READY FOR MODEL 3

Maybe you're one of the hundreds of thousands of people who are already on the Tesla Model 3 reservation list. Or maybe you haven't plunked down $1000 yet, but are getting ready to do so. Or maybe you're trying to better understand Model 3 so you can make a decision after your current auto lease runs out, or when the car you currently own begins to show its age.

No matter which of those categories best describes you, I think that *Getting Ready for Model 3* will provide you with guidance about electric cars in general, about the Tesla Model 3 in particular, and about the things you'll need to consider and do as you prepare to take delivery of your first *battery electric vehicle* (BEV).

### Model 3

Sure it's still a car, but Model 3 is different in a variety of ways. Let's begin by exploring a few of them.

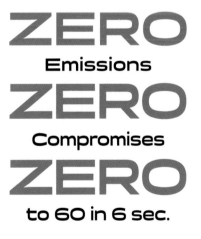

First, it's a *battery electric vehicle* (BEV), and that means it has a number things that you won't find in conventional, *internal combustion engine* (ICE) cars. For example:

- There's a big battery that provides the power for Model 3
- There is no internal combustion engine. Model 3 is not a plug-in hybrid vehicle.

The Telsa Model 3

- The energy required to keep the big battery full comes from the electric grid, not from fossil fuels. And the source of electricity from the grid is becoming environmentally cleaner with each passing year.

- There are no buttons, knobs, or switches. Almost all mechanical controls have been replaced with software generated icons on a large, touch-sensitive, landscape display.

In addition to what's not there, here are some things that are:

- An *electric motor* powers Model 3. Electric motors are really quite simple and very reliable. For Model 3, the electric motor serves to drive the vehicle's wheels, but it also transforms itself into a generator that recharges the big battery as you bring the car to a stop.

- All cars have significant amounts of software (apps) that control internal functions (e.g., fuel consumption, braking, even collision avoidance), but Model 3 software is special. Because Model 3 has its own

> **@evannex_com Model 3 isn't your dad's Audi; it's not even your older sister's Prius or your Cousin's Volt. It's different, and you need to understand why. #UniqueCar**

IP address, it accommodates *over-the-air* (OTA) software updates. Tesla Motors can and will upgrade software functionality during the life of your car, meaning that Model 3 will get better as time passes.

Second, because Model 3 is a BEV, there are many, many things that will be missing (in a good way) when you trade your current conventional ICE vehicle for Model 3.

For example:

- There won't be any oil changes—ever!

- You'll *never* have a transmission problem, because Model 3 doesn't have a transmission.

- You won't have to top off your anti-freeze, because Model 3 doesn't have a radiator.

- The amount of vehicle service is reduced because there are fewer parts and therefore fewer things to go wrong.

- You won't ever have to stop at the gas station, unless you need a candy bar or a restroom.

The Model 3 Reveal

Third, you'll own a 21st century car for the first time. The level of tech associated with the Model 3 is a significant departure from the tech provided with conventional (ICE) vehicles. Here are a few examples:

- As I noted earlier, all of the things you used to do with a combination of buttons, knobs, switches are now done with an iPad-like touch screen. That means that your car can be upgraded to offer more features and functions.

- Because Model 3 can receive OTA updates, it gets better with time. Not only interaction, but things like improved internal vehicle systems controls, more robust autonomous driving features, and improved battery management.

- Speaking of autonomous driving, Tesla Motors has indicated that Model 3 will come with a sensor suite that will allow it to be outfitted with hardware and software options that enable the car to drive itself, first with your help, but ultimately on its own. In the extreme, that means you'll go to a sporting event or rock concert (where parking is diffucult and expensive). Your Model 3 will drop you off, drive itself to an appropriate off-site parking area, and then pick you up when you summon it after the event.

> **@evannex_com A 21st century car isn't defined by its 20xx Model year; it's defined by the tech it delivers to make your driving experience better. Model 3 delivers stellar tech. #21stCenturyCars**

There's obviously a lot more to understanding Model 3 and a lot more tech to be discussed. You'll learn much more about the car, about its design, and about its features, options and variants in the chapters that follow.

## Some Background

The Model 3 is the culmination of a long-term strategy defined by Tesla CEO, Elon Musk. In 2004, he invested in a struggling start-up named Tesla Motors. His strategic goal wasn't to build an electric car—rather it was to build cars that were the best in their class and just happened to be electric. He felt, correctly it turns out, that if EVs were demonstrably better cars than their gasoline-powered counterparts, a significant market would evolve and grow.

An EV word cloud

Elon's strategic plan was to begin with a high performance, limited edition sports car, the Roadster, that would demonstrate that EVs didn't have to be stodgy, or ugly, or uninteresting. The Roadster set the stage for the next element of his plan—the development of a premium sedan that would be the best in its class. Model

S was the result of that work, and today, a variation called Model X is being characterized as the best SUV/crossover on the market.

With the know-how and revenue generated by Models S and X, Musk began work on a mass market BEV—The Model 3. Again, his intent wasn't to build an affordable electric vehicle. Rather, it was to build the best small sports sedan on the planet (that just happens to be electric). Based on the phenomenal response to Model 3, it looks like he succeeded.

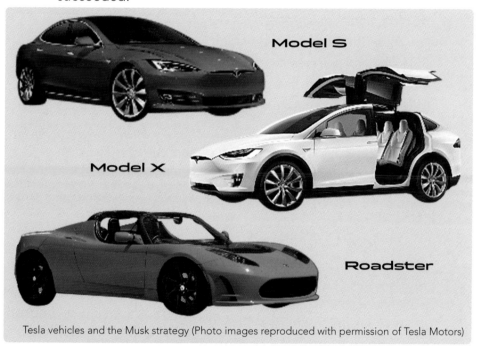

**Model S**

**Model X**

**Roadster**

Tesla vehicles and the Musk strategy (Photo images reproduced with permission of Tesla Motors)

## Elementary EV Concepts

Many drivers have absolutely no clue what happens under the hood of the conventional automobile, and yet they love their cars and use them effectively every day. The same holds true for some EV owners, although I suspect that a higher percentage of EV owners have at least some idea of what's going on.

In honesty, there's no real need to develop a deep understanding of the underlying technology to own, drive, and enjoy Model 3 or any other BEV.

But it's nice to have a basic understanding, so that you won't be snowed when you encounter BEV jargon and won't feel like a dummy when a friend asks a simple question.

In addition, it's likely that your family, friends, co-workers, and acquaintances will want to talk once they learn you're on the Model 3 reservation list or are considering a BEV. They'll have questions about the battery, about how electricity gets from the grid into your car, about whether Model 3 is nothing more than a fancy Prius. You should be able to answer those questions.

**The Battery.** It's reasonable to state that the battery lies at the heart of every electric vehicle. That's why it's important to understand the battery and the way your Model 3 battery is charged.

In his best selling book, *Owning Model S*, Nick Howe[1] provides an excellent battery and charging metaphor that is wholly appropriate for the Model 3. Think of the Model 3 battery as a bucket that you can fill with water. The bucket can be empty, full, or partly full. Charging Model 3 (or any other BEV) is a lot like filling the bucket. When you drive Model 3, it's a lot like emptying the bucket. Of course, you don't actually fill the battery with water, you fill it with electricity. Obviously, the electricity doesn't come through a water pipe, but rather from the electric grid, then into your

1. Howe, Nick, *Owning Model S*, second edition, Evannex, 2015. Available through www.evannex.com

house, through a plug into your charging cable, and finally into your Model 3.

**Volts and Amps.** I know, I know, volts and amps can be confusing. But again, Nick Howe comes to the rescue.

So, if you try to plug your Model 3 into a 110v electrical circuit (a common household circuit in the United States), electrical "pressure" will be low and electricity will flow slowly. The lesson to be learned is that low voltage (pressure) results in slow flow of electricity, which means that the battery in your Model 3 (your "bucket") will fill slowly when you charge it.

The moral of this metaphor? It's far better to increase the "pressure" of your charging circuit so that charging will be faster and more efficient. For that you'll need a 240-volt (or more) circuit. More on that and everything it implies in Chapter 5.

> **@evannex_com** Nick Howe explains: "Volts are like water pressure. If pressure is high, water will shoot out of a hose at great speed. Likewise, the higher the voltage, the faster electricity will flow. #Fill'R-Up

But what about amps? Continuing with Nick's metaphor, amps are a measure of electrical current and are analogous to the volume of the water that comes out of the hose. The more amps, the more current that flows through a particular circuit.

**Kilowatts and Kilowatt-Hours.** Whenever Model 3 (or any other BEV) is discussed, you'll likely hear people taking about kilowatts and kilowatt-hours. A *kilowatt* (1000 watts) is a measure of power. But it's also a measure of how quickly you fill your battery. A *kilowatt-hour* (kWh) is a measure of capacity—how big the bucket is, or discarding the metaphor, how big your battery is.

So, the bigger the BEV battery measured in kilowatt-hours (kWh), the greater the capacity of the battery. And the greater the capacity of the battery, the farther your Model 3 can go without a charge.

**EVs.** The descriptor "EV" (electric vehicle) has become increasingly popular throughout the auto industry. It gives a car an environmentally conscious patina and at the same time, creates the appearance that a company that predominantly builds and sells ICE vehicles is also in the mix for electric vehicles. Appearances can be deceiving. Any car that uses a battery, coupled to an electric motor to power its drive wheels, even if it also uses an internal combustion engine and gasoline for most of the miles traveled, can be termed an "EV."

Today, there are *hybrid vehicles* that use a small battery to power driving at low speed and for short distances. The battery is charged from a gas engine that is used for the majority of all travel. There is no plug-in capability. A variation of the hybrid, called a *plug-in hybrid* electric vehicle (PHEV), uses a somewhat larger battery that can be charged from the grid. The PHEV battery provides power for an electric motor that can drive the car for distances that typically range from 20 to 60 miles. When the battery drains, a gasoline-powered ICE takes over for the remainder of the travel.

When an automobile jettisons the ICE entirely, leaves fossil fuels (i.e., gas, or natural gas, or diesel) behind and relies solely on a battery and electric motor(s) to power the vehicle, you have the holy grail, a battery electric vehicle (BEV). Here's a table that outlines the characteristics of some existing BEVs, including Model 3.

Most BEVs fall into the "city car" category, small cars with relatively small batteries and limited range. Today, vehicles built by Tesla Motors sit at the apex of the EV world.

| Bev | Range (miles) | HP | Acceleration (0-60 mph) | Top Speed (mph) | Cost $ |
|---|---|---|---|---|---|
| Ford Focus Electric | 76 | 143 | 10.1 | 84 | 29,170 |
| BMW i3 | 81 | 170 | 7.0 | 93 | 42,400 |
| Volkswagen e-Golf | 83 | 115 | 10.1 | 87 | 28,995 |
| Fiat 500e | 93 | 111 | 8.7 | 85 | 31,800 |
| Kia Soul EV | 93 | 109 | 9.2 | 90 | 31,950 |
| Mercedes B-class, B250e | 101 | 177 | 7.9 | 101 | 41,450 |
| Nissan Leaf SL | 107 | 107 | 10.2 | 100 | 36,790 |
| Chevrolet Bolt | 200 | 200 | ~7.0 | 91 | 37,500 |
| Tesla Model 3(RWD) | 215 | - | <6.0 | - | 35,000 |
| Tesla Model S (AWD) | 265 | 691 | 2.8 | 155 | ~90,000 |
| Tesla Model X (AWD) | 275 | 763 | 3.2 | 155 | ~95,000 |

The BEV market circa 2016-2017

They provide battery capacity, range, and performance (not to mention good looks) that are unchallenged by any other automotive manufacturer. There is little question that BEVs from other manufacturers will emerge over the next five years, but the notion that any one of them will be a "Tesla Killer" is nonsense.[2]

Model 3 exemplifies a BEV that is affordable and at the same time, provides battery capacity, range, performance, and timeless design that will remain unchallenged for a number of years.

The Model 3 Reveal (Photo © Kyle Field, 2016, courtesy of Clean Technica)

## Getting Ready

If you've read this far, you've actually begun your preparation for Model 3. You now have a general understanding of Model 3 and a grasp of basic BEV terminology and concepts. That's all well and good, but what are some of the things you should begin thinking

2. If you would like to learn about the BEV landscape, see: Pressman, R., "The Footprint of a Tesla Killer," Seeking Alpha, Jan 11, 2016, available at: http://seekingalpha.com/article/3802096-footprint-tesla-killer

about now, even though it's likely your Model 3 won't be delivered for quite some time?

There are two things that are worth considering right now—your personal driving habits and the way in which you're going to create a "personal charging infrastructure." Your *personal driving habits* encompass everything from the distance you commute to work, to where your friends and family members (e.g., grandparents, parents, siblings) live, to your propensity for spur-of-the-moment, long distance road trips, to whether you're an aggressive driver or not. A *personal charging infrastructure* will help you to think through how you'll provide electricity to charge your battery—there are many, many options and one approach isn't necessarily right for everyone.

> @evannex_com **There's plenty of time to get ready for Model 3, but start thinking about it now! #GetReadyForM3**

We'll consider "getting ready" in much greater detail in later chapters.

# CHAPTER 2
## WHAT WE KNOW ABOUT MODEL 3

The Tesla Model 3 reveal happened on March 31, 2016, and in the immediate aftermath, some obvious questions were answered, and a lot more about the car was implied. In this chapter you and I will take a look at what we know about Model 3 and how that information implies still other vehicle characteristics. We'll also discuss what we don't know.

### The Overall Design

In a blog post at the Evannex website,[3] Matt Pressman writes:

> Even the Detroit News,[4] home team paper to GM, Chrysler, and Ford admits the Tesla Model 3 is, "the most intriguing auto story since the Model T, and Elon Musk is the boldest American auto entrepreneur since Henry Ford."

"The boldest entrepreneur since Henry Ford" and his designers and engineers created a Model 3 design that is stunning, not just for a car at a $35K base price, but for any sports sedan at any price point.

**BOLD** Strategy
**BOLD** Pricing
**BOLD** Car emerges

That's an amazing thing to say, because in most cases, $35K conventional ICE cars are easy to spot—the design is often derivative and the look tells you that you're near the bottom of a premium manufacturer's line-up. For example, why would BMW provide a design aesthetic for its 3-series in a way that would make folks say, "Hey, this car is so, so cool, I really have no interest in the 4-series or the 5-

3. Pressman, M., "Why Model 3 is Changing Automotive History," evannex.com, April 27, 2016, available at: http://evannex.com/blogs/news/116450437-why-tesla-model-3-is-changing-automotive-history-video

or the 6- or 7-series. Manufacturers leave design elements on the table, so that you'll come back when you get a little older and a little richer and buy up.

Elon Musk at the Model 3 Reveal Event, March 31, 2016

But the Model 3 reveal told a different story. Tesla Motors designed a car that stands on its own. Sure, it's in the same vehicle class as the BMW 3-series or the Audi 4-series, but the look, the tech, and the feel doesn't say, 'I'm an entry level car.' It does say, "I'm a serious sports sedan with a design and feature set that back up that statement."

*Motor Trend*[5] took a look at Model 3 a few weeks after the reveal. Here's what their people thought:

"It looks much better in person; pictures don't do it justice," said *Motor Trend* staff photographer Robin Trajano, without one trace of irony. "The proportions don't really work in pictures but in person looks really good. I wouldn't mind owning one."

His boss, *Motor Trend's* visuals manager Brian Vance, went for specifics, "It really does have a lot of his Mazda concepts in it, like the lines." Vance is referring to Franz von Holzhausen, Tesla's head of design, who was at Mazda prior to joining the company. "I can't believe the entire roof is glass. It's two pieces (three if you count the windshield) but in the right light, looks like one piece."

Video producer Travis Labella quipped, "My first impression? That I'm going to be seeing a lot of these on the road very soon. It's the future. It's my kind of future."

Our always thoughtful Reynolds remarked that the Model 3 is a "well-metered blend of classical automotive cues and future-car fantasies. The nose has attitude and its flanks are streaked with athletic, visual tendons — but it's the tall greenhouse and glass-bubble roof that will define this car. This is not another slot-window

4. Payne, H., "Why I'm Buying a Tesla Model 3," Detroit News, available at: http://www.detroitnews.com/story/opinion/columnists/henry-payne/2016/04/05/payne-buy-tesla-model/82682524/

sedan saying 'Don't see me.' The Model 3's square yards of glazing shatter that isolation, opening you to the whole, passing world. Taken together, it's this new visual vocabulary for the modern electric car.

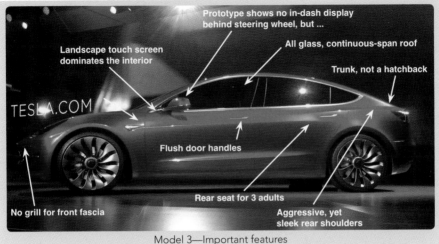

Model 3—Important features

Let's take a look at what we know about the Model 3 design.

In the annotated photo above, I've tried to summarize the important exterior design features (and a few important interior design features) of Model 3. Let's consider the most important aspects.

**Profile.** The chopped rear and long, sloping nose give the car an aggressive look that is a welcome departure from the boxy looks of the BMW 3-series or Audi 4-series. The Lexus IS-series has a bit of this look, but Model 3 outdoes them all.

If Model 3 were an ICE vehicle, its exterior design shape would dictate cramped rear seating (because of the long nose and the need to place the front seats behind a firewall), but because it's a BEV, Model 3 has a lot more space to work with (more on that when we discuss the interior).

**Nose.** If you think about it for a moment, many premium cars are identified by their grilles—the BMW "kidney bean" grille is a signature feature of every car in the company's inventory. A four-ring logo inside an inverted trapezoid

5. "Go Behind the Scenes at Our Model 3 Shoot," *Motor Trend*, available at: http://www.motortrend.com/news/tesla-model-3-behind-the-scenes/

identifies a car as an Audi. As usual, Tesla Motors decided to go a different way with Model 3.

@evannex_com **The Model 3 profile puts the car in motion, even when it's standing still. #AmazingLines! #GetReadyForM3**

The no-grille front fascia (nose area) is a controversial design feature for Model 3. The slightly bobbed nose (in profile) has taken some criticism—one automotive reviewer called it "fugly" while others seem unsure. Dozens of make-overs have been suggested at the Tesla Motors Club forum, but it appears that the nose design is here to stay. I lean towards

@evannex_com **Yes there's no grille, and the car doesn't 'smile' ...But you certainly will! #About Fascia**

commenters who argue that the nose has a Porsche-like look to it. That's certainly a compliment for a car in this price range.

The Model 3 nose—a no-grille front fascia

The Model 3 nose design is easier to fabricate (one metal stamping) and has fewer parts, connectors and complexity than a typical grilled fascia. Bottom line, it's less costly, and because Tesla Motors has committed to the $35K base price, less costly is good.

There's another possible reason for the bobbed nose. As you'll learn in Chapter 4, the range of a BEV is very important, and one of the most important factors that affect range is "drag"—the degree to which a car moves through the air in front of it. Some argue that the slight nose bob helps Tesla to achieve a remarkable drag coefficient of 0.21. I'll discuss drag in greater detail in Chapter 4.

Because Model 3 is a BEV, it doesn't need to breathe in the same way that a conventional car does. After all, there's no radiator, no fuel injection system, no anti-freeze, no hoses, just a small opening at the air dam (the lower portion of the front fascia) to allow airflow to cool the battery.

**Glass roof.** When I had my test ride in Model 3, it was night, but even so, the roof is startling. It's almost as if you're in a convertible, but without the wind noise. But the roof is more than aesthetics. The enormous windshield dips low to the hood (there is no instrument cluster in front of the steering wheel, but more on that when we discuss the interior). There is a structural cross member at the B-pillar location that separates the front glass windshield from the rear glass, but otherwise, the roof represents a panoramic view of the sky.

There are a few concerns about the glass roof. If a stray rock bounces up off the road, hits your Model 3 windshield, and cracks it, replacement cost for this vast expanse of glass will not be cheap. Luckily, almost every auto insurance policy covers windshield glass without a deductible. In addition, a glass roof may become a problem in climates where the sun is always strong, causing the interior to heat up more than it normally would.

There is some legitimacy to the first concern—replacement will undoubtedly be costly but covered by insurance. But my experience driving a Model S with a panoramic glass roof in South Florida indicates that the second concern is minor at best. Tesla Motors treats its Model

S roof glass with special materials that reduce visible light by over 90 percent and heat by approximately 80 percent. In Florida, the glass roof attenuates both light and heat quite well. More importantly, it's very likely that the roof glass for Model 3 will be treated in the same way.

Model 3 glass roof  (Photo © Kyle Field, 2016, courtesy of Clean Technica)

It's questionable whether the glass roof will be standard equipment for the base Model 3, even though some have suggested that it will be. My guess is that by the time Model 3 goes into production, the glass roof will be an extra cost option with a solid roof being provided as standard equipment.

**Door handles.** It's a small thing, but door handles matter. If they're flush to the vehicle they reduce aerodynamic drag (more on that in Chapter 4) and for Model 3, that means increasing the range of the vehicle, however slightly. For the Tesla Model S, the door handles were a crowd pleaser, extending when the handle was touched and retracting later. However, relatively expensive mechanisms were required to achieve this, so Model 3 uses a simpler approach.

The Model 3 door handles are flush to the body and are shaped like a stylized truncated J lying on its side. You push the wide part of the J and the handle rotates outward to allow the door to be pulled open. When you let go, the handle rotates back to the flush position.

The interior door handles are implemented as shaped buttons on the interior door pull, but because the interior was prototypical, it's difficult to

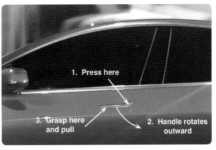

Model 3 door handles

say whether these will make it into the production Model 3.

**Vehicle size.** Although there is no official indication of the actual dimensions of Model 3, Tesla co-founder and CTO J.B. Straubel has been quoted as saying the base dimensions for Model 3 are about the same as an Audi A4. If that's the case, then approximate size might be 186' L x 73" w x 56 " H (4.72 m x 1.85m x 1.4m).

However, future Model 3 owners have other ideas. An Instagram poster, @bobarchibob (architect, Bob Schatz) did a simple analysis of a Model 3 profile photo, and based on a projected wheel size of 20 inches, he comes up with the profile dimensions noted in the following figure. Using Bob's photographic analysis, Model 3 is about 168 inches (4.25m) in length with a 115-inch wheelbase.

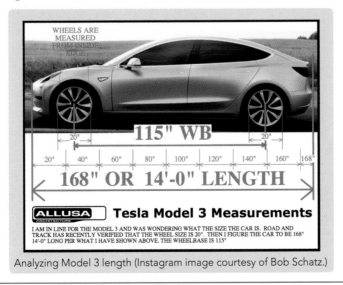

Analyzing Model 3 length (Instagram image courtesy of Bob Schatz.)

**The Skateboard.** Model 3 will use the same "skateboard" design (shown in the photo that follows) as the Model S and X. Because the exterior dimensions of the car are directly proportional to the dimensions of the battery, some have speculated that Model 3 base battery capacity will be in the 60 to 70 kWh range, leading to the advertised base 0-60 mph time of about 6.0 seconds. However, *Electrek*[6] reports that Tesla's Vice-President of Investor Relations, Jeff Evanson stated that the base Model 3 will be offered with a battery pack option smaller than 60 kWh. This can be achieved because Model 3 will be considerably lighter than Model S and will also have a lower coefficient of drag.

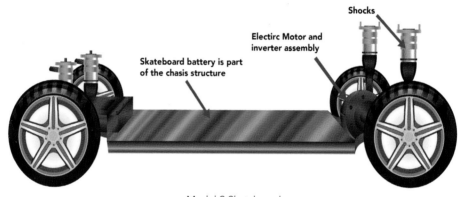

Model S Skateboard

However, regardless of battery pack size, Tesla Motors is not sacrificing quickness with Model 3. During the reveal, Tesla CEO Elon Musk confirmed that Model 3 will have a 0-60 mph time of under six seconds. And, when asked on Twitter[7] if an upgraded version of Model 3 will have Tesla's lightening-fast "ludicrous" mode, Musk responded, "Of course."

## The Drive Train and Motor(s)

The base Model 3 is a rear-wheel drive (RWD) car. But even the RWD version of Model 3 will have excellent traction on snow and ice due to control software that provides super-quick torque response when one rear wheel begins to slip. It should be noted that Model 3, like all BEVs, does not have

6. "Tesla confirms base Model 3 will have less than 60kWh battery pack option, cost is below $190kWh and falling" *Electrek*, available at: http://electrek.co/2016/04/26/tesla-model-3-battery-pack-cost-kwh/

a conventional transmission, but rather uses a much simpler gear reduction drive and a variable speed electric motor.

The photo below depicts a Model S RWD motor and drive train. The elements depicted remain, but based on Elon's graphic presentation of Model 3 (including 3-D CAD drawings) during the reveal, it appears that the entire subsystem (motor plus drive train) has been reduced in size significantly.

A dual motor, all-wheel drive (AWD) version of the Model 3 will undoubtedly be available at extra cost. The AWD Model 3 will provide improved quickness, better range (because it will probably have a larger battery), and definitely better road handling. In the AWD version, control software looks at wheel traction every 1/100 of a second and will implement torque vectoring to reduce wheel slip on wet, snowy, or icy roads.

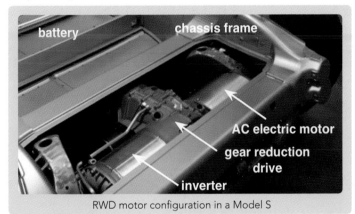

RWD motor configuration in a Model S

## The Interior

We have all become accustomed to seeing a small sports sedan and assuming that rear leg space will be cramped and interior volume will be tight, if not claustrophobic. That's because conventional cars operate under a number of significant constraints. The most important is the internal combustion engine—big, heavy, and a volume hog in the front of the car.

7. https://twitter.com/elonmusk/status/726210827699806208

Because front volume is taken up by the ICE and the firewall (to protect you from the engine, just in case it ... well ... never mind), the front seats must be positioned back in the car. The problem is that the rear seats can only move backward so far because of a downward sloping roofline, if the car is to have a sporty look. That means cramped legroom in the back seat.

**Volume.** Interior volume for Model 3 is anything but cramped. I'm 6'2" (1.88m) tall and during my test ride, I sat in the rear seat of Model 3. My knees were about 8 inches (20 cm) from the back of the front seat and the top of my head was about 2 - 3 inches from the glass roof. The reason for my rear seat comfort is illustrated in the following drawing. If you look closely at the drawing, you'll note that the front passenger seats have been shifted forward. This is easily accomplished because there is no need for a conventional firewall structure. Therefore, the driver and passenger have plenty of room, but the seats they occupy are moved closer to the front of the car.

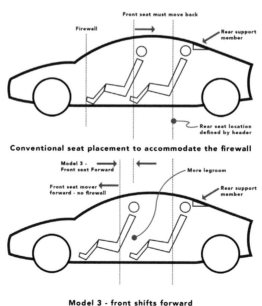

Front and Rear for Model 3

That provides good legroom for backseat passengers, but to achieve enough headroom for tall, backseat passengers something had to give. That something was described by Elon Musk in a tweet, "Only way to get enough rear passenger headroom was to remove the rear roof cross-car support beam."

And because there is no "rear roof cross car support beam", Model 3 is not a hatchback even though it looks like one. That's because there is no structural member to which a hatch could be hinged. Instead, Model 3 has a conventional trunk—roomy, but not as big as a hatchback trunk. It's important to note, however, that the rear seats of Model 3 do fold down, allowing you to place long objects through the trunk and into the passenger compartment of the car.

> @evannex_com **Model 3 is not a hatchback. Unfortunate? Maybe, but Model 3 makes up for it with copious interior room for passengers.**

Like all solid designs, compromises were made. In this case, headroom trumped trunk space.

**Frunk and Trunk.** The front trunk (the "frunk") for Model 3 is relatively small, but still provides sufficient space for one or more small items or a small suitcase. The trunk, as I have already noted, is hinged approximately mid-way up the rear window. It provides adequate, but not voluminous, storage when the seats are in the upright position.

**Design.** Overall, the interior shown during the Model 3 reveal was prototypical. It's likely that there will be significant changes

to the steering wheel, the dash and center console area, the seats, and other interior appointments. For example, early design sketches of the Model 3 interior showed a u-shaped steering wheel, something that would be a significant departure for conventional cars. In a tweet, Elon Musk stated in his typical showman-like fashion: "Wait until you see the real steering controls and system for the 3. It feels like a spaceship.[8]"

**HVAC.** During my test ride at the Model 3 launch event, a Tesla engineer indicated that traditional heating/venting and air conditioning (HVAC) vents would not be used and would be replaced by long venting slots that run along the bottom of the windshield and under the dash. Details are sketchy, but expect something new.

**Display Tech.** As I got into Model 3 and glanced at the 'floating' 15-inch landscape display, I couldn't help conjuring the image of a display found in aircraft. Every vehicle function (e.g., speed, battery level, all controls, 'buttons/knobs/swtiches', the nav system, as well as all other apps (e.g., audio, phone) is displayed as part of the touch screen landscape display. A quick glance behind the steering wheel indicated that there is no instrumentation display in the "binnacle" area (the area behind the steering wheel)—none at all. Part of this goes to a future in which the Model 3 will drive itself autonomously (more on that in Chapter 7). There's no need for a speedometer or other instrumentation behind the wheel.

But I think there's something else. The demographic that will buy Model 3 has grown up using digital smart-devices and is comfortable with the manipulation of imagery and information using everything from a smartphone to a tablet to a smart watch. Model 3's floating, landscape display is simply an extension

> @evannex_com **The Model 3 display is aircraft-like. The fact it seems to float in space makes it very device like, and at night, slightly spacecraft-like.**

8 "Available at: https://twitter.com/elonmusk/status/716729420078133248

of that. In addition, the landscape display is equally accessible to both the driver and the passenger—it is not directionally biased toward the driver.

Model 3's landscape display.

Because there is no instrumentation behind the steering wheel and because the display 'floats' from a cantilever support, the dash does not need to accommodate the display and has been lowered to aid in visibility and roominess.

It's worth mentioning that some observers believe that the lack of an instrument cluster behind the steering wheel might be a harbinger of a "heads-up display" in which all relevant driving data is projected onto the lower portion of the windshield glass. Elon Musk has alluded to the lack of an instrument cluster as "making sense" after "part 2 of the Model 3 unveil." But I think there may be another intriguing possibility, and I'll get to it in a moment.

Many interior functions that are not addressed by the touch screen might be implemented with a series of controls integrated directly into the steering wheel. In fact, the conventional controls for lane change and wipers may disappear and be replaced by paddle like controls or buttons on the steering wheel itself.

> **@evannex_com With the landscape display, Model 3 becomes still another smart device that you'll use. #IDrivemycomputer**

But here's what I think might be happening, and it is a rather intriguing possibility. The empty space behind the steering wheel might not be empty after all. It could be filled by three HD video displays driven by one rear facing center camera and two rear-facing side view cameras on the driver and passenger sides of the vehicle. These would replace the rear view mirror and side view mirrors (assuming Tesla Motors can get consent to do so from the NHTSA) with video cameras that would provide visual output for the driver and also provide image recognition input for the autonomous driving system. By the way, eliminating the side view mirrors might very well be one of the secrets that will enable Tesla to achieve a remarkably low 0.21 coefficient of drag.

I think it can be argued that side view camera displays behind the steering wheel are both more effective and much safer than the conventional approach. The driver would not have to swivel her head—a dangerous activity that takes eyes off the road. Rather, the driver simply lowers her eyes slightly to see one or both side views. These views could (hypothetically) be initiated by a button push on the steering wheel, available only when desired.

In addition, removing the rear view mirror solves an installation and aesthetic issue posed by the extremely large

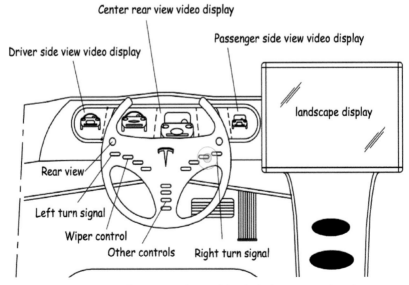

An intriguing refinement to the Model 3 dash design (speculative)

windshield glass.

**Sensor Tech.** Model 3 will have a sensor suite that will make it ready for autonomous driving. To achieve this, Tesla is reported[9] to be working on a "next generation sensor suite" that will be more powerful and less expensive than existing tech.

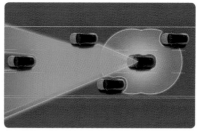

Autopilot sensor zones (Image reproduced with permission of Tesla Motors)

Tesla Motors is working with Mobileye, a small Israeli company, to develop the hardware (sensors) and software required for next generation (next-gen) sensors. *Electrek*[10] reports that "… currently Tesla's Autopilot enables automatic steering on highway, automatic lane-change through the turn signal, self-parking and automatic emergency steering/braking. The company plans on releasing more features through over-the-air updates utilizing the same hardware, but the system, which consists of a forward-looking camera, a radar, and 360 degree sonar sensors, is limited by its hardware suite."

> **@evannex_com Your Model 3 will 'look' everywhere at once. As a consequence, your car may very well drive itself … safely. #LookMaNoHands**

The likely next-gen sensor suite for Model 3 will rely more fully on specialized, multiple cameras with sophisticated image recognition software. The CEO of Mobileye implied that the NextGen autonomous system for Tesla vehicles might include as many as eight cameras, forward-looking radar and an array of ultrasonic sensors around the vehicle.

I'll discuss autonomous driving in more detail in Chapter 7.

**Seats.** Because the Model 3 interior that I experienced during a test ride was prototypical, it's difficult to assess the quality or even the structure of the seating (with the

9. See: http://www.fool.com/investing/general/2016/02/28/model-3-to-sport-next-generation-tesla-motors-inc.aspx
10. See: http://electrek.co/2015/11/02/supplier-hints-at-next-generation-autopilot-hardware-for-tesla-as-soon-as-2016/

exception of front to back placement). The seats in the Model 3 test cars had heavy bolsters normally found in expensive performance cars. It's unlikely that these will find their way into the base Model 3, but I wouldn't be surprised if they're found as an extra cost option in performance versions of the car.

Prototype seats for Model 3

## Battery

Most of us are more accustomed to discussions about 2 liter engines or 452 HP muscle cars, but relatively few people have any feel for a car that has a ~60 kWh battery.[11] In fact, most people have no clue what a kilowatt-hour (kWh) is! Of course, you do, because you've read Chapter 1.

In Chapter 1 you learned that Model 3 is a battery electric vehicle (BEV). That means that it doesn't use gasoline as

11. The approximation symbol (~) is used because Tesla has not yet announced the battery size for the standard Model 3. Some believe it will be in the 45 to 50 kWh range, while others think 60 kWh.

a power source—ever. By the way, that also makes it radically different from other "EVs" like the Chevy Volt, or the Toyota Prius, or the head-turning BMW i8. Each of those cars is a plug-in hybrid, using a small battery for relatively short distances and then switching over to a gasoline engine to drive longer distances.

> @evannex_com **Gasoline has 100x the energy density of a Lithium ion battery, BUT electric motors are 80% efficient, while an ICE is 20% efficient. #ElectricMotorsRule**

Not Model 3. Because it's a BEV, all of its energy is stored in its battery. The bigger the battery, the more energy available to Model 3. At its base price, it's likely that the Model 3 will have a ~60 kWh battery[11]. More expensive versions (i.e., faster and with more range) will have a larger battery.

If the Model 3 battery is architecturally similar to the battery Tesla has built for the Model S and X (and that's very likely), it's actually composed of thousands of lithium-ion cells. Each cell will be built individually (at Tesla's "Gigafactory") and forms a complete battery. The cells are then connected together as one addressable unit, called a *module*. Based on an evaluation of various comments and images presented at the reveal, it's

> @evannex_com **Does the Model 3 have one big battery or lots of little ones? Uh … both. #BatteryTech**

likely that the Model 3 battery will use eight battery modules (as opposed to 14 for Model S and X) and that the size of the individual cells will be larger. Finally, modules are organized into a pack so that they can be controlled by a *battery management system*—the BMS. The BMS addresses a variety of operational concerns that keep the battery efficient and safe.

You also learned in Chapter 1 that the larger the battery, the greater its storage capacity (in kilowatt-hours) and the more energy storage capacity, the greater the range.

## Range

The base Model 3 is projected to have an EPA-rated range of 215 miles. That means that under a set of EPA-dictated conditions Model 3 can be driven for approximately 215 miles before the battery runs out of energy to power the electric motor. It's the equivalent of an empty gas tank for a conventional ICE vehicle.

The following chart represents BEV range for a variety of BEVs. City cars (e.g., Nissan Leaf, Ford Focus Electric and offerings from BMW, Volkswagen, Fiat and others) typically provide 60 to 110 miles of range. The Chevrolet Bolt offers range touted at 200 miles. The Tesla Model S and X provide between 220 and 300 miles of range. The base Model 3 is touted at 215 miles of range with the clear implication that variants of Model 3 will provide greater range.

Range is just a number, but a very important one. One of the problems with any discussion of range is that many parameters affect it. A broad combination of environmental conditions, your personal driving

@evannex_com **Range is just a number. YMMV, literally. #RangeDepends**

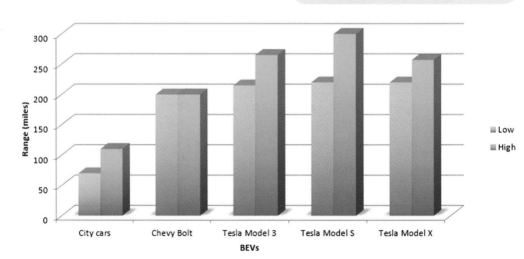

Low and high range values for BEVs

habits, the terrain over which you drive, and other factors come into play.

There's also an emotional component to any discussion of range. Because BEVs are powered by a battery, and most people have experienced a dead smartphone, everyone, including future Model 3 owners understands that a battery can go dead if it is not recharged. And because there's a perception that recharging is difficult (it isn't), future owners of Model 3s might experience "range anxiety"—the sometimes irrational fear that they'll be stranded without a charge. I'm going to discuss range and range anxiety in much more detail in Chapter 4.

Range Anxiety

## Regen

*Regenerative braking*, nicknamed "regen," is a characteristic of BEVs that catches the uninitiated by surprise. When you take your foot off the Model 3 accelerator, the car will begin to slow down almost immediately (it feels a bit like a smooth downshift for those of you who are familiar with manual transmissions). This occurs because the electric motor is transformed

> **@evannex_com** Give me a brake? Model 3 gives you a brake without any action on your part. It's called "regen." #BrakesNORegenYES

into a generator when power from the battery is removed (remember, you took your foot off the accelerator). The motor turned generator produces an electric current that is sent back to the Model 3 battery to recharge it.

At first, regen takes some getting used to. Based on your experience with ICE vehicles, you expect the car to coast once you remove your foot from the accelerator. Your Model 3 will not do this (although it's likely, but not advisable, that you'll be able to turn regen off). Instead, regen kicks in, and your car will "brake" without

you having to touch the brake pedal. Braking will be gentle, but noticeable. After about a week of driving, you'll be totally used to the phenomenon, and after a few weeks, you won't know how you lived without it.

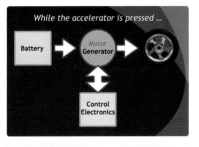

For those who want to understand how you can generate energy during braking, think back to what your high school science

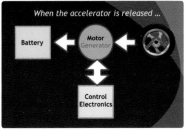

teacher called "kinetic energy" (KE) — the energy that any object (including a car) possesses when it is in motion. For a car, energy is required to accelerate the car and maintain its speed.

When the Model 3 electric motor receives electrical energy as input from the battery, it converts the energy derived from an electromagnetic field into mechanical energy transmitted by the motor's rotor. This provides *torque* —rotational force — that causes the drive wheels of a vehicle to rotate. Stated more succinctly, if input to the motor is electrical energy, output will be mechanical rotation or torque. But if the electrical input stops, the mechanical rotation derived from the KE is used as input. The motor becomes a generator and produces electrical energy as output. Model 3 slows as KE is transformed into electric output, and regenerative braking occurs.

## Performance

Little is actually known about the performance and handling characteristics of base Model 3. My test ride in the car was conducted in a dual motor, all wheel drive, high capacity

battery, high-performance version of Model 3. Therefore, it's a bit difficult to discuss the performance and/or handling of the base model, which will likely have a single motor and different performance and handling characteristics.

Model 3 performance (Photo © Kyle Field, 2016, courtesy of Clean Technica)

The car that I rode in (dual motor, all wheel drive) accelerated in much the same way as a Model S—by that I mean it was extremely quick and smooth, pushing you back in your seat as the car took off from the standing start. Road handling was impressive as Model 3 went through a small slalom course as it returned to the Tesla Design Center. Cornering was tight, braking was impressive with little nosedive, and as I mentioned, acceleration was awesome.

> @evannex_com **Even the base Model 3 will be 'hot,' the performance version(s) will be awesome! #Model3Performs**

Confirming my impressions, here's what *Road and Track*[12] had to say about their test ride experience:

> How'd it drive? My wheelman wouldn't give any details about our car's drivetrain, other than to reveal that it was a dual-motor all-wheel-drive setup... [possibly] providing enough juice for Ludicrous-mode all-wheel-drive launches and 0-60 in under four seconds.
>
> I don't know if that's the drivetrain I sampled. But from the back seat, on a short stretch of road closed off for the Tesla event, the Model 3 launched with ferocious grip and absolutely zero drama. It wasn't quite the chest-collapsing wallop of a Model S P90D in Ludicrous mode,

12. Sorokanich, B., "Tesla Model 3: Brief On-Road Impression of a Performance Model," *Road and Track*, April 1, 2016, available at: http://www.roadandtrack.com/new-cars/first-drives/news/a28677/2017-tesla-model-3-p80d-brief-driving-

but without a stopwatch, I'd say the Model 3 I rode in zipped from a dead stop to 75 mph a bit quicker than a Subaru WRX STI—silently.

Sadly, there was no place to get a good impression of the Model 3's steady-state handling or lateral grip, but our driver zig-zagged through a handful of quick slalom maneuvers. The Model 3 stayed nearly flat, with plenty of grip. Credit Tesla's low-slung platform, which puts the mass of the batteries (and in this case, the dual motors) as low as possible in the package.

Whether any of those characteristics translate into the base Model 3 is an open question. But if the base Model S is any indication, even the lowest price version of Model 3 will be an impressive sport sedan.

## Safety

Tesla Motors prides itself on building the safest cars on the planet. In fact, the Tesla Model S has received a five-star safety rating from both the U.S. NHTSA and the Euro NCAP. Tesla Motors[13] reports:

Of all vehicles tested, including every major make and model approved for sale in the United States, the Model S set a new record for the lowest likelihood of injury to occupants. While the Model S is a sedan, it also exceeded the safety score of all SUVs and minivans. This score takes into account the probability of injury from front, side, rear and rollover accidents.

The Model S has the advantage in the front of not having a large gasoline engine block, thus creating a much longer crumple zone to absorb a high speed impact. This is fundamentally a force over distance problem – the longer the crumple zone, the more time there is to slow down occupants at g loads that do not cause injuries. Just like jumping into a pool of water from a tall height, it is better to have the pool be deep and not contain rocks. The Model S motor is only about a foot in diameter and is mounted close to the rear axle, and the front section that would normally contain a gasoline engine is used for a second trunk.

Model 3 will likely exhibit the same vehicle architecture described by Tesla Motors in the preceding paragraphs. As a consequence, it is likely that it will be the first moderately priced sports sedan that will achieve a five-star safety rating in every category tested by the NHTSA.

13. See: https://www.teslamotors.com/blog/tesla-model-s-achieves-best-safety-rating-any-car-ever-tested

In a compelling example[14] of what a 5-star safety rating and an outstanding crumple-zone design means in the real world, tragedy was avoided in Germany when 5 teenagers traveling (way too fast)  in a Tesla Model S lost control of the car, went airborne for over 80 feet, landed nose first, and then rolled over, totaling the vehicle. Some of the occupants sustained serious injuries, but none were life-threatening. Had the teenagers been in an ICE vehicle, the nose-first landing would have rammed the engine back into the passenger compartment with tragic results.

> @evannex_com **Model 3 can take a punch … and allow you to walk away. #SafetyFirst**

The Model S architecture saves lives. The Model 3 architecture will do so as well.

14. Gitlin, J.M, "Tesla's inherent safety saves five joyriding teenagers in Germany," Ars Technica, May 9, 2016, available at: http://arstechnica.com/cars/2016/05/teslas-inherent-safety-saves-five-joyriding-teenagers-in-germany/

# CHAPTER 3
## PROBABLE MODEL 3 VEHICLE CONFIGURATIONS

When I was in Los Angeles for the Model 3 launch event, I traveled from my hotel at LAX to the Santa Monica Tesla store. My intent was to wait in line to sign-up for Model 3. I arrived at a little after 8:00am, two hours before the store would open. The line was already 150-people long. I stood and chatted with a number of 20-, 30-, and 40-somethings as we waited. This allowed me to conduct an admittedly unscientific survey of the young-buyer demographic for Model 3.

When I mentioned that I was a Model S owner, smiles brightened and questions started to flow. They asked whether I loved the car (yes), how it differed from conventional cars (in many ways), whether it was as fast as they've read (uh huh), how much maintenance it required (very little), and whether I'd do it again (absolutely).

Each person I spoke with was to be a first-time EV owner although one young woman drove a Prius hybrid. Each was generally unfamiliar with BEV basics, but nearly everyone said that the $35K price points was "doable" in their situation, although some said that they'd have to begin saving now.

**Many** Options
**Many** Decisions
**Many** Model 3 Variants

As is the case for all newbies to the BEV world, there was a lot of concern about range. I got lucky and predicted (before the reveal) that range would likely be 215 or 220 miles and explained why. Nearly everyone was satisfied with my response and when I asked whether they'd pay for more range, I got responses like this one: "It would be nice, but not if it costs too much."

Something interesting happened when we began to talk performance. Some of my new Tesla friends really didn't care about quickness or road handling at all. They just wanted a sleek, zero emissions vehicle. Impressive zero to 60 times elicited some responses like, "Nah, that's not for me."

But another cohort within my unscientific sample was right out of the *Fast and Furious* crowd. "Man, I'm up for a 4 second zero to 60 ... and I'll pay to get it," said one young man as a number of people smiled and nodded their heads.

But at that point, all of these things and the decisions they implied were pleasant abstractions. It would be a long time until the first Model 3 was delivered.

## Configuring Your Model 3

It won't happen right away but it will happen. You'll get a long-awaited email from Tesla Motors with the following subject line: **Subject: It's time to configure your Model 3**

You'll smile and post on Twitter or Instagram, celebrating the end of a very long wait. But after receipt of this email, and a visit to Tesla's on-line Model 3 Design Studio, you'll have to begin making decisions about the actual Model 3 configuration that you'll be ordering. In this chapter, I'll talk about some of the decisions that you'll have to make, and also give you an indication of how people on the Model 3 reservation list will likely configure their Model 3s.

Like almost all moderately priced cars, Model 3 will be sold with a variety of options and upgrades that will surely increase vehicle cost, but also improve everything from range to the ability to use a Tesla supercharger. In addition, options that dramatically improve vehicle performance and enable autonomous driving features are also likely. Finally, you'll also have the ability to choose from a menu of nice-to-have features and functions.

> **@evannex_com So many Model 3 options, so little … er, so much time to decide what you want. #OptionsMatter #DecisionsDecisions**

No one yet knows the precise list of Model 3 options and upgrades, but it's fairly easy to make a list using the options and upgrades available for other Tesla Motors vehicles. There is, of course, no guarantee that every upgrade and option discussed in this chapter will be offered for Model 3, but it's likely that you'll get to configure your car with a reasonably large subset of the options noted here.

## Color

The Model 3 color palette is still under wraps.[15] But if the premium Tesla Motors vehicles are any indication, the colors offered will be relatively predictable and conform to colors offered by most manufacturers—black, white, grey, red, silver, blue, and maybe a few wildcard colors. There has even been some discussion of a matte black paint color.

Matte finish Model 3

---

15. If you'd like to see what Model 3 will look like with Tesla's existing palette of colors, visit http://www.model3config.com/ for an unofficial look.

Elon Musk noted on Twitter, "Matte black was surprisingly popular. Probably makes sense to bring it to production."[16] Options might also include more expensive 'metallic' paints.

Car color is very personal, and I'm sure you'll anguish over it before pulling the trigger. If at all possible, try to see the colors in natural light on a sunny day before you make your choice. A color that looks blah in a picture might really pop when the sun hits it at all the right angles.

In case you were wondering, *Wikipedia*[17] provides an interesting breakdown of the most popular car colors in North America, Europe, Asia and Worldwide. Automotive paint manufacturers PPG Industries and Dupont conduct polls that indicate (unsurprisingly) that white, silver, black and grey are the most popular colors in the United States and worldwide. About 70 percent of all cars purchased are chosen in those colors.

There will certainly be other Model 3 colors, but if you're a bit of a rebel and want something really different, some Tesla owners are opting for vinyl wraps that provide a selection of thousands of colors. So, if you absolutely, positively must have a neon blue Model 3, order the car white and get it wrapped!

## Battery Size

Because the size and range of the base Model 3 are now known, it is possible to estimate the battery size for the base model. It's likely that the standard battery will be ~60 kWh range. A battery of that size will provide the announced range

16. https://twitter.com/elonmusk/status/716701798002610176

17. Wikipedia, "Car Clor Popularity, available at https://en.wikipedia.org/wiki/Car_colour_popularity

of 215 miles and acceleration of 0 - 60 in under six seconds.[18] But what if you have interest in a Model 3 that delivers more range, say 260 to 300 miles and 0 – 60 acceleration in the four-second range? There will be a Model 3 for you.

It's extremely likely Tesla Motors will offer at least one larger battery size, possibly in the ~75 kWh range. This optional larger battery would be used for all dual motor variants of the Model 3 and for all performance variants as well.

Model3tracker.info (h/t: Teslarati[19]) has begun to collect crowd-sourced polling data from people who are currently on the Model 3 reservation list. Based

> **@evannex_com Even if you don't think you'll need it, access to Tesla's supercharger network is a good thing to have. #Supercharged**

on responses from almost 2000 reservation holders, you can gain some insight into likely options choices for future Model 3 buyers. Fully 75 percent of people who responded indicated that they would opt for the larger battery. *Ka Ching!*

## Supercharging Capability

If you travel long distances via the interstate highway system, you'll need the capability to recharge your vehicle at Tesla superchargers. Supercharger access will be provided, but it will be part of an extra cost package for the base Model 3. In my opinion, this option is a no brainer. Sure, it will add to the cost of the base model, but it's a must-have.

Model S at Tesla supercharger facility

18. As I mentioned earlier in the book, others suggest that a smaller battery in the 40 – 50 kWh range can still achieve the designer range and acceleration.

This appears to be reinforced by Model3tracker.info crowd-sourced polling. Almost 90 percent of those on the Model 3 reservation list say they will opt for a supercharger access option. *Ka Ching!*

## Single or Dual Motor

The base Model 3 will likely have a single motor and rear wheel drive, but it's also very likely that an optional dual motor, all-wheel drive variant will be offered. If Tesla's premium Model S and X provide us with meaningful indications (and I believe they do), the dual motor variant for Model 3 will offer higher performance, will be potentially more energy efficient, thereby resulting in greater range, and will provide considerably better road handling characteristics.

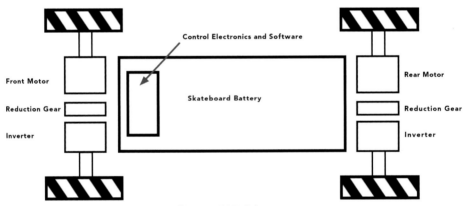

Dual Motor AWD Schematic

Model3tracker.info crowd-sourced polling indicates that the dual motor option is quite popular with future owners. About 77 percent indicate they would pay for an all-wheel drive, dual motor option. I suspect, however, that this number might trend downward significantly once the added cost of dual motor option for Model 3 is better known.

In a series of tweets in the days following the Model 3 reveal, Elon Musk indicated that the cost of the dual motor, AWD option will be "less" than $5,000. *Ka ching!*

19. Liu, Gene, "Early Insight into Tesla Model 3 Most Popular Configurations," Teslarati, April 14, 2016, available at: http://www.teslarati.com/early-data-tesla-model-3-popular-configurations/#r1JSsHthDIArGVhg.

## Performance Options

Additional quickness and improved road handling will be available as options for Model 3, but they will cost. First, it's likely you'll have to opt for the bigger battery as well as the dual motor, AWD option. *Ka ching!* A performance package might include an improved suspension, bigger tires and wheels, a bundled trim package (both exterior and interior) and pay-for-play hardware and software upgrades that will enable your Model 3 to achieve "ludicrous[20]" mode. *Ka ching! Ka ching!*

No one yet knows the cost of these options, but they will add substantially to Model 3's base price. The need (want?) for range and speed can be satisfied, but the cost might be fairly steep.

> **@evannex_com If you want a high performance Model 3, you'll need a bigger battery, dual motors, other performance upgrades, and some extra cash. #NeedForSpeed**

As I noted earlier in our discussion of Single or Dual motor cars, Model3tracker. info crowd-sourced polling indicates that a substantial majority (over 75 percent) of future Model 3 owners has indicated that they would pay for a dual motor option, and by extension, for the performance improvements implied by that option. Interestingly, Model3tracker.info indicated that fewer than one quarter of all reservation holders would purchase a "performance" option, and fewer than 15 percent would opt for something like an "insane" mode speed upgrade.

Model 3 accelerating  (Photo © Kyle Field, 2016, courtesy of Clean Technica )

20. Tesla CEO Elon Musk was asked on Twitter whether Model 3 would have "ludicrous" mode in its performance versions. His response, "Of course." Discussion at: http://gas2.org/2016/04/30/tesla-model-3-will-ludicrous-option/

There appears to be significant interest in improved suspension with over 40 percent of Model3tracker.info respondents indicating that they would be willing to purchase such an option as part of an improved handling package.

## Roof Options

Some writers have suggested that the glass roof may itself be an option and that a more conventional metal roof would be part of the base Model 3. Others have posited that there may be an optional panoramic sunroof. At this stage, all of this is pure conjecture, although it is interesting to note that more than half of the Model3tracker.info respondents indicated that they would opt for an all glass roof. Having experienced it first hand, I can tell you that it is very cool, and for aesthetics and bragging rights alone, the all glass roof might be worth an upgrade cost.

The Model 3 all glass-roof (Image reproduced with the permission of Tesla Motors)

## Autonomous Driving Features

Based on comments made by none other than Elon Musk, Model 3 will have a complete sensor suite (albeit, not enabled) as part of every Model 3. To enable the sensor suite, you'll have to select and pay for a semi-autonomous "autopilot" driving option. *Ka ching!*

It's as yet unclear as to the extent of autonomous driving functionality that will be offered for Model 3. Will autonomous driving functions

enable the car to drive itself in a parking lot or parking garage, on city streets, on the highway? Could you summon it from across town or across the country? No one yet knows.

But future Model 3 owners are intrigued by the capability. According to Model3tracker.info, almost 90 percent say they would opt for autonomous driving functions as an optional extra. *Ka Ching!*

## Wheels and Tires

To my eye, wheels (along with a beautiful body design) make the car. Tires keep it on the road and help improve both performance and ride. The prototype wheels that were part of the Model 3 reveal may or may not be part of the Tesla's wheel offerings, but you can bet on two things: (1) standard wheels will be smaller diameter and slightly less sexy than any extra-cost, optional larger diameter wheels offered by the company, and (2) the standard wheels will have hints of Tesla's signature "turbine" look.

It's quite likely that at least some of the optional wheels will be available in matte grey or gun metal, and that a matte black finish isn't out of the question.

| Model 3 "Custom" Wheels | Turbine wheels for Model 3 | Model 3 "Aero" wheels |

Larger diameter wheels will require low profile tires and must be viewed as an aesthetic option, rather than a functional requirement. From the standpoint of wear, tire and rim damage in areas that have potholes, and lack of harsh ride, small diameter wheels and corresponding tires are the best choice. But big rims and wide tires look *really, really* good. The choice will be yours.

Model3tracker.info indicates that under 20 percent of reservation holders would opt for large diameter wheels—a somewhat surprising result until you realize that large wheels can add $3,000 to $4,000 to the sticker price. *Ka Ching!*

## Interior Appointments

The Model 3 interior is a work in progress, so it's a bit difficult to speculate on interior options. Here are some of the possible option choices for Model 3:

**Upholstery and Trim.** If Tesla Motors follows precedent established for Model S and X, upholstery and trim options will be limited—at least at the beginning of production. You'll probably have a choice of three upholstery colors and 3 to 5 trim finishes. The much-discussed "vegan" interior may be an option.

It's likely that the "performance" version of Model 3 will be available with one or more additional trim finishes (e.g., carbon fiber) and possibly, a different color for the head liner.

> **@evannex_com** Much is yet unknown about the Model 3 interior. The 'reveal' interior was a rough prototype. #InteriorUnknown

**Seat Types.** The standard seat design for Model 3 will be comfortable and well appointed. But it's also quite possible that you'll be able to upgrade to "performance" seats that have larger side bolsters, and possibly, air vents for heating and/or cooling.

**Sunshades.** Because of the massive glass front windshield, it will be interesting to see what Tesla will offer in the sunshade category and how the sunshades will be implemented within the Model 3. The Model X has an enormous front windshield as well and currently uses sunshades that rotate out from the upper A-pillar. It's possible that Model 3 will use the same approach. The type of sunshade option you can choose will be a function of the roof option for your vehicle.

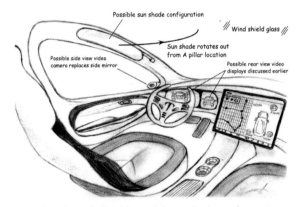

Artist's rendering of possible sunshade configuration

**Front Seat Center Area.** It appears that Model 3 will come with an integrated center console,[21] but the base version may have a rather bare interior that lacks that amenity. It's also possible that Model 3 will reproduce the "cubby" that can be found in both the Model S and X under the 17-inch portrait display. However, because the 15-inch landscape display will undoubtedly be standard across all versions of Model 3, the cubby would have to be reconfigured to fit the new dash design.

**Sound System.** Again, looking to a precedent set by Model S and X, a "premium sound system" option is almost a certainty for the Model 3. Whether or not this upgrade is right for you depends on your musical ear. Model3tracker. info data show that just over 35 percent of reservation holders would opt for the premium sound.

21. Our very first product at EVANNEX was a center console insert (CCI) developed exclusively for Model S. I designed and built the first one in my garage while I waited for my car to be delivered. For its first 3.5 years of production, a center console was not standard in Model S. Tesla might decide to do the same thing for Model 3.

### Landscape Display

It's likely that the hardware configuration will be standard for all versions of Model 3. However, it's entirely possible to have optional software upgrades that provide more versatile apps, better graphics, and more information than that provided with the base version of the car.

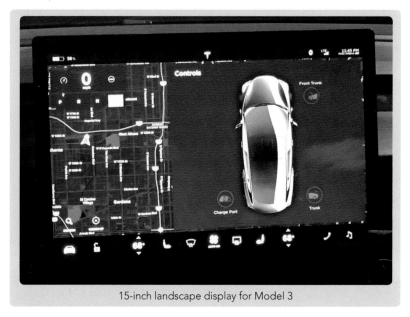

15-inch landscape display for Model 3

### Winter Package

If you live in the northern parts of North America and Europe, this option is well worth considering. Approximately half of all Model3tracker.info respondents indicate that they'd consider it.

### Other Upgrades

Options in this general category include things like special interior lighting packages, headlight options, a towing package, a bicycle hitch, and other minor upgrades as yet undefined.

Unless you're really stretching financially to purchase or lease the base Model 3, it's likely that you'll choose to purchase one or more of the configuration options discussed in this chapter. You'll balance needs, wants, and your wallet and come up with a vehicle configuration that is the best combination of all three.

# CHAPTER FOUR
## RANGE AND RANGE ANXIETY

Every car has a finite supply of onboard fuel (e.g., a gas tank typically holds around 15 - 18 gallons of fuel), and therefore, every car has limited range. But because gas stations are everywhere, there's no worry when the fuel gauge of an ICE vehicle approaches "E." Unless, of course, you're on a desolate road far from civilization—and your fuel gauge shows empty.

*Where's the next gas station,* you think nervously, *Can I get there before I run out of fuel?*

The emotion you feel is called *range anxiety.*

I suspect that more than a few future Model 3 owners are experiencing it vicariously as they think about their exciting new BEV.

But why the anxiety? Because there's no place to charge? Actually—*no!*

Here are a few facts to dispel that notion for those of you who aren't yet tuned into the BEV world.

# More
## Range
# More
## Certainty
# Less
## Range Anxiety

By the time Model 3 hits the streets, there will be over 40,000 public charging locations in the U.S.—in parking garages, shopping malls, RV parks, entertainment locations, hotels, and many other venues. In fact … you can plug-in anywhere there's an electric outlet you have permission to use.

If you're a Model 3 owner, there's great news. Currently, there are 617 supercharger stations across North America

with 3,652 individual chargers. Tesla Motors has committed to double the size of its North American Infrastructure to about 1200 supercharger stations by the end of 2017—just in time for the first Model 3 deliveries. For example, today Tesla Model S or X owners can drive cross-country using superchargers to "fuel" their road trip, and do it at no cost! However, in some areas you might need to detour from a faster route in order to reach the closest supercharger.

But by the time you get  your Model 3, you'll be able to travel to most places within North America using Superchargers with relative ease along major highways. That means that in less that 30 minutes, you can add

150 – 170 miles of range to your Model 3, plenty of charge to get to the next supercharger station after another two hours of driving. You'll have access to the supercharger infrastructure—although access will not be free-of-charge for Model 3 owners.

But what if you're away from an interstate? There are smartphone apps such as Chargepoint, Plugshare, or Recargo that will help you find the nearest public BEV charging location, no matter where you are.

And remember, most of the time you charge your Model 3 at home, every night. You wake up and your car is "full" every single day. Bloomberg Business[22] comments on BEV charging:

As it turns out, charging isn't as big a hurdle as many drivers imagine. Sure, there are still roughly 13 gas stations for every public charging location. But that's ignoring the most common type of charging station of all: your garage. About two-thirds of U.S. homes have them. With an at-home charger and 215 miles of range, most customers rarely need to stop at a charging station. Looking at it that way, charging locations already outnumber gas stations by about 400 to 1.

Public charging stations are primarily needed for drivers who spend long stretches on the road at a time—be it for road trips or business travel. For most of these drivers, it's the speed of the chargers—not the absolute number—that matters most, so Tesla is focusing on building a charging network with the fastest chargers in the world. Tesla Superchargers can provide 170 miles of driving range in 30 minutes, and owners of the Model X and S can use them all without charge. The number of Superchargers will double this year alone, according to Tesla.

The preceding facts should allow you to dismiss range anxiety or at least downgrade its importance and impact in your mind. But anxiety is often driven by emotion, not facts, so for some future Model 3 owners, it will be very real—at least at the beginning.

> **@evannex_com ICE owners aren't obsessed by "range." But then again, they have gas stations on every corner. #RangeAnxiety**

In this chapter we'll discuss range so that you better understand it, and then revisit range anxiety so that you can better deal with it … if it's bothering you.

## Range

Range is the distance you can travel in your Model S with a battery that is fully charged. More specifically, range is a function of:

- A specific set of vehicle parameters and the manner in which the vehicle is driven
- A specific set of driving conditions that include external factors associated with the vehicle's surroundings

22. http://www.bloomberg.com/news/articles/2016-04-21/tesla-changed-cars-forever-now-it-must-deliver

The vehicle parameters that affect range are not exclusive to BEVs. In fact, they affect the "mileage" of every ICE vehicle and therefore, the range of every car.

Model 3  (Photo © Kyle Field, 2016, courtesy of Clean Technica)

**Vehicle Parameters.** With respect to Model 3, vehicle parameters are the specific characteristics of the vehicle and the way you drive it. For example, as the speed of Model 3 increases, it will experience more "drag," and that results in more force required to move it through the air. The more force required, the more your battery drains, and therefore, the shorter your range.

Vehicle design dictates the external shape of the car, which in turn affects the way the air flows over the vehicle's surfaces, which affects "drag," that affects the force required to move Model 3 through the air.

Finally, the battery matters—a lot! The base Model 3 will have a high capacity battery pack. And higher cost versions of the car will have still larger

@evannex_com The faster you drive, the shorter your range. That's true whether you own Model 3 or an ICE vehicle. #SpeedKillsRange

battery packs. The higher its capacity, the more energy can be stored in the battery and the greater the vehicle's range.

**Speed and Acceleration.** Model 3 looks fast. It's performance, even for the base model will be quite good, and that will entice more than a few Model 3 owners to push the car just a bit. As someone who has been accused of having a lead foot, I get it. But be warned. All of us who drive fast reduce the range of our vehicles. That happens whether you have an ICE car or a BEV.

In the context of this discussion, it's important to make a distinction between speed and acceleration. In general, speed has a significant impact on Model S range, but acceleration doesn't. That may come as a bit of a surprise.

Model 3 accelerating (Photo © Kyle Field, 2016, courtesy of Clean Technica)

Over the years, you've heard that hard driving—that is, rocketing away from a stoplight—will kill the mileage in an ICE vehicle. It's only natural to assume the same holds true for BEVs. But it's not.

The internal combustion engine (ICE) is generally inefficient and because it produces torque along a curve (not instantaneously) only after you slam the accelerator, a lot of fuel is required to build up enough torque to make the car accelerate quickly. That's why hard acceleration kills mileage for an ICE car.

But that's not the case for BEVs like Model 3. The reason is that electric motors have extremely high efficiency and produce instantaneous torque from a dead stop. That means the motor in your Model 3 doesn't have to work especially hard to get your car moving fast. Nick Howe[23] discusses this in the context of the Tesla Model S, when he writes: "The amazing efficiency of the electric motor means that driving 70 vs. 50 has a much bigger impact on range than accelerating from 0 – 60 in 4 seconds vs. 8 seconds." To descend into the technical weeds for a moment, that's because the force required to propel the vehicle forward at a steady-state speed increases as the square of the velocity.

> @evannex_com **Quick acceleration from a standing stop won't affect range very much, but continuous high speed will. #FastOffTheLine**

Like most things in life, speed vs. range is a trade-off. If you want to get there fast, you will reduce your range. If you have to go a long, long way, reducing your speed helps to improve your range.

To illustrate, consider this estimated Speed vs. Range graph for Model S (blue) and Model 3 (red).

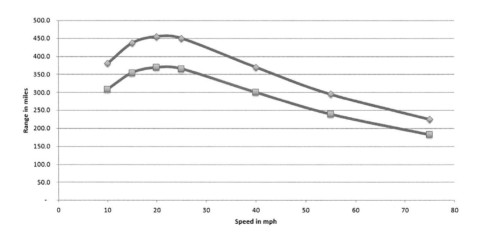

Speed vs. Range (for the Model S (blue) and Model 3 (estimated in red)

23. Howe, N., *Owning Model S*, second edition, EVANNEX, 2015, available at: www.evannex.com

At very low speed, Model 3 range (the red curve) will be greater than the vehicle's EPA rated range. In extreme cases, "hyper-milers" have achieved about 70 percent greater range than the EPA rating for a BEV. For Model 3, that would mean that you can travel about 370 miles on one battery charge if you hold your speed to about 20 mph, drive where there are few, if any, stops, and travel in areas that do not have hills or a headwind. That's unrealistic, so what can you expect for Model 3's real world range?

If you drive 55 mph with few if any stops, your range will be somewhere between 215 and 240 miles (for the base Model 3) with favorable environmental conditions (e.g., no hills or headwind). At 75 mph,[24] your range will drop to approximately 20 percent to about 180 miles. And if you drive over 80 mph, range will drop still more. Based on my real world experience with Model S, your actual results may be slightly lower.

**Drag.** Earlier, I mentioned that exterior design is a vehicle parameter that has a significant impact on range. Anything about the vehicle design that reduces "drag" increases range. But what is drag?

Without getting too technical, drag is the degree to which an object resists moving through the air as a force is applied to move the object forward. Objects with a low "drag coefficient" are slippery and move through the air more easily than objects with higher drag coefficients.

Model 3 will have the lowest drag coefficient of any production car, 0.21. By comparison, the Tesla Model S has a drag coefficient of 0.24, the Chevy Corvette ZR-1 has a coefficient of 0.28, and the $2.1 million Bughatti Veyron sports

> @evannex_com **Slippery cars require less energy to push them forward. Slipperiness is implied by a low drag coefficient. Model 3 is very slippery. #SlipSlideTakingARide**

24. Please be certain to follow all posted speed limits.

a drag coefficient of 0.36! Hundredths really do matter when the drag coefficient is considered so Model 3's 0.21 is remarkably good.

How did the Tesla's designers do it? Although there is a lot more to it than a bulleted list, the designers optimized the Model 3 body shape by achieving these results:

- reduced drag area—the front facing area that is impacted by airflow as the vehicle moves forward, measured in square feet or square meters.

- minimized external attachments, such as roof racks, an antenna, a large spoiler and the like

- improved side mirror profile, which surprisingly, can reduce drag by as much as 2 to 7 percent, or eliminate them entirely by providing side view video cameras

- reduced air turbulence around and below the vehicle

- improved fabrication details (e.g., panel gaps, wheel design)

InsideEVs.com[25] Steven Loveday reports on comments made by members of the simulation software company that Tesla and other automakers use to analyze airflow around a vehicle body. He writes:

> … when Tesla reduced the Model S [drag coefficient] from 0.32 to 0.24, the range increased by 50 miles. Ales [the digital simulation expert] speculates that the 0.21 reduction could add another 10-20 miles of range [to Model 3].
>
> … The first noticeable change is the fact that the Model 3 has no grille. This allows for the continuous wedge shape to aid in air flow. Some people complained about the look of this, but the all-electric car has no need for it.
>
> Ales believes that there are no "active" aero devices on the Model 3; another cost saver. Instead, everything is designed to be aerodynamic in and of its own physical design. For instance, all wheel designs use a "turbine-blade" style that forces air beneath the car, limiting drag.

25. Loveday, S., "Tesla Model 3's aerodynamics explained by EXA's digital simulation expert," April, 28, 2016, available at: http://insideevs.com/tesla-model-3-aerodynamics-explained-by-exas-digital-simulation-expert/

Since Tesla decided not to switch to cameras yet,[26] the side mirror mounts are thinner and more aerodynamic. Air is forced to flow into the front of the car and over the wheels, due to air curtains in the fenders. This also directs the air flow more smoothly along the sides of the vehicle. Underneath the vehicle has not been seen clearly, but Ales said it is likely to be "flat and smooth" with a diffuser at the rear.

Airflow Simulation (Photo © Kyle Field, 2016, courtesy of Clean Technica)

**The Battery.** The Model 3 battery must provide the energy necessary to generate the torque (rotational force from the electric motor) required to push a Model 3 through the air. Therefore, a natural question is, why can't Tesla Motors build higher capacity, cheaper batteries, therefore allowing the Model 3 to have an even greater range?

A detailed answer to that question is beyond the scope of this book, but a quick discussion will help you better understand the challenges Tesla Motors faced as it designed the Model 3 battery.

As you now know, Model 3 uses a skateboard design in which the battery acts as a structural member for the car's chassis. Therefore, the geometry into which the battery can be placed is limited.

**@evannex_com Battery tech is complicated and difficult. That's why your smartphone doesn't run 7 days on a single charge. #KnowYourBattery**

When Tesla Motors designs its batteries, it must consider six parameters that represent constraints on the design:

- specific energy—also known as the capacity of the battery
- cost—the overall manufactured cost per kWh
- life span—the number of charging cycles that the battery can accommodate
- performance—the ability to operate effectively in various climates
- safety—reducing any danger of the battery overheating during charging, and
- specific power—the ability of the battery to deliver on-demand current when needed.

Mountain Road negatively affects range

**Environmental factors.** The design of Model 3 and its battery capacity are the dominant factors that affect the range of the car, but there are other environmental factors that also affect range. Most of these are out of your control, but they do matter.

- The direction and velocity of the wind can have an immediate effect on range. That's simply common sense. If you're driving into a strong headwind, more force is required to move the car forward, and range is affected.
- The same goes for the terrain you're driving over. If it's hilly or mountainous, range will be affected, possibly as much as 30 percent in extreme situations.

- Temperature effects are more subtle, but very cold weather can have a significant affect on the battery, and therefore, on range. In fact, it can reduce range by as much as 20 – 30 %

> **@evannex_com** If **you live in a cold weather climate, expect your Model 3 range to be negatively affected in winter. #ColdHurtsRange**

- Finally, anything (like a roof or bicycle rack) that you attach to the exterior of Model 3 can have an effect on range—and that effect is almost always negative.

**Other Suggestions.** In addition to the topics we've discussed, plugincars.com offers these suggestions for improving the range of any BEV:

- Check your tire pressure—rolling resistance can affect range
- Look for travel routes with small gradients and few intersections
- Schedule your charging to stop just before you begin driving—this reduces the likelihood of any small loses that may occur as the car sits idle with a full charge
- Give yourself more time, resulting in relaxed driving and more effective use of regen

## Range Anxiety

At the beginning of this chapter I suggested that range anxiety is driven as much by emotion as by any real fear that you'll actually run out of battery charge. To begin, think about your driving habits. Using the United States as an example (other countries have similar characteristics), it's likely that you drive less than 50 miles round trip to work each day. In fact, 65 percent of Americans fall into that category. Only 8 percent drive more than 120 miles round trip for their commute. This histogram on the following page shows average one way commuting distance in miles (horizontal axis) and the percentage of drivers who travel that distance (vertical column).

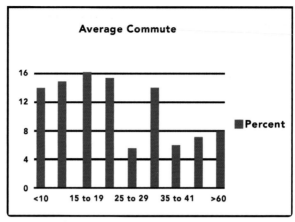

Percentage of drivers and their average one-way commute distance

Regardless of the battery option you choose, your Model 3 should be able to handle your commute with absolutely no problem. But if you're going to use your car for more than commuting, your other driving patterns do matter. Consider these questions:

> @evannex_com **Everyone's driving pattern is different. It's worth doing a self-evaluation. #PatternPerfect #LifeMapping**

*How long is your daily commute along with daily errands?* If your commute is only a small part of the miles you drive each day, you should order a Model 3 with sufficient battery capacity or plan to charge at your destination, before heading home.

*How far do you drive for entertainment purposes?* If a weekly round trip to a cabin in the woods is 180 miles, you'll need a place to charge your Model 3 at the cabin and possibly, along the way.

*How far away is your extended family and how often do you visit?* If grandma's house is 90 miles away, you'll have to be sure that grandma has a place for you to charge your car once you arrive, if you drive 70 mph+, unless there's a supercharger along the route.

*Do you take long road trips (vacation, family visits, etc.)*

on routes that don't use the interstate highway system? If you take 200+ mile road trips to places that are not within easy distance of Tesla superchargers, you probably should consider ordering a Model 3 with greater range.

It's worth emphasizing that by the time you take delivery of your Model 3, long trips will be much more manageable with respect to range.

- As I mentioned earlier in this chapter, the Tesla Supercharger network will be built out and cover almost all of the interstate highway system and then some.

- A growing network of destination chargers at hotels, shopping malls, parking garages and other sites will be much more robust that it already is.

- Public J1772 chargers offered by municipalities and the federal government can provide a partial recharge in a few hours.

- As I'll discuss in the next chapter, it will become increasingly likely that your place of work might also have charging capability for your Model 3.

Last, it's important to note that it's likely (based on "Trip Planner" software updates that have occurred for Model S and X) that Model 3 will also have trip planning software built directly into the navigation system. What does this mean? Basically, that your Model 3 will alert you to all Tesla Superchargers that are located along your planned route. You'll always be alerted if charge is running low, and you'll be shown the way to the closest Supercharger or Destination Charger. The "Trip Planner" software has been designed to ensure you always have enough charge to get you to your destination.

Overall, range for Model 3 is an issue. You may have to do a little planning when you take

**@evannex_com Range is an issue for Model 3, but not as big a one as many people believe. #RejectRangeAnxiety**

long trips and possibly allocate a little more time to account for charging, but overall it's really no big deal. And range anxiety? In fact, it's a non-issue most of the time and can be managed in the instances when your Model 3 doesn't have the range you need for a long trip.

So ... be calm ... and carry on.

# CHAPTER FIVE
## CHARGING YOUR MODEL 3

I haven't walked up to a gas pump and placed the nozzle into my personal vehicle in over four years! Sure, I do it for an occasional rental car, but the entire activity now seems both inefficient and quaint. The process for filling my Tesla Model S is considerably more intimate—I charge the car every night when I get home. I plug it in just as I plug in my phone or notebook computer. In the morning, the car, the notebook, and the phone are all fully charged.

You'll use exactly the same process when you take delivery of your Model 3. But now is the time to begin thinking about what I call *personal charging infrastructure* (PCI). In most cases, you'll create a PCI at your place of residence—in your garage if you own or rent a house or condo with one; at your parking spot, if you live in a residence without a garage. Creating a PCI is really quite simple, if you're the only person who has to approve the project, but if you live in a communal setting—a condo, an apartment building, a co-op—things can get a bit more complicated and sometimes, quite frustrating. And if you live in a city and use on-street parking? Then what?

## Many
### Options
## Many
### Decisions
## Many
### Model 3 variants

In this chapter we'll discuss how to create a PCI for a variety of different living arrangements, but before we do, let's spend a few pages talking about public charging infrastructure. Why? Because for a small, but non-trivial percentage of future Model 3 owners, a *public charging network* (PCN) may be the only reasonable approach for getting a charge.

## Public Charging Networks (PCNs)

Most industrialized nations have established a national EV infrastructure program that includes charging stations along major roads, in many cities, and at shopping locations, stadiums, hotels, and other public facilities.

In the United States, we have no national program, but as you already know, Tesla Motors has shown that the private sector can create a large and effective BEV charging infrastructure (superchargers). By the time your Model 3 is delivered, Tesla superchargers will be accessible almost everywhere in the United States, in most European countries, in Australia, and across much of Asia.

**Superchargers.** One of the reasons that Tesla's supercharger network is so attractive is that it allows you to charge your Model 3 very quickly—something that other PCNs do not accomplish very well. You can easily get the electrical equivalent of 150 - 170 miles of range added to your battery in about 20 - 30 minutes. In that time, refuel yourself with a beverage, a snack, and a stop in the restroom. After that, just check your Tesla app, and it's likely that in that short period of time, your Model 3 will be fully charged.

Tesla app during Charging

Many less capable PCNs provide charging at a rate of 24 to 30 miles per hour of charging. Quite useful if you're spending a fair amount of time at the charger location (e.g., if the charger is at your workplace or at a hotel you'll be staying at), but difficult if you're in transit to another destination.

The Tesla supercharger network has been designed to accommodate travelers, and Tesla frowns upon its use as your local/daily charger. It's really poor EV etiquette to use a supercharger for your daily charging needs, thereby creating a potential bottleneck for other Tesla owners who are traveling. Not cool!

> **@evannex_com Tesla superchargers are the best PCN you can use, but there are other PCNs, lots of 'em. #ChargerHunting**

**Destination chargers.** In addition to Tesla superchargers, you'll have access to one of a number of charging networks, independently operated "destination" chargers at malls, hotels, parking garages, municipal buildings, and the like. Also, there are a growing number of businesses that have installed chargers for use by their employees. For these types of chargers, all of which can be used (with appropriate adapters) for Model 3, there are three models: (1) pay-as-you-go, (2) monthly subscriptions, and (3) free-of-charge.

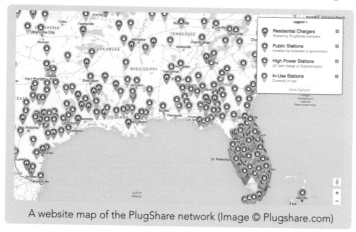

A website map of the PlugShare network (Image © Plugshare.com)

Tesla has its own "Destination Charging" network that is growing even faster than its supercharger network. Tesla's destination charging network is not as fast as a the supercharger network but it's still fast compared with other public charging options. Your Model 3 onboard "Trip Planner" software will also alert you to Tesla's Destination Charging options along your planned route. This can be especially handy because they're often located in hotels, restaurants, and shopping malls that make good places to stop along the way.

To determine which public charging network elements will best meet your needs, follow these recommendations, suggested by plugincars.com and adapted for use in this book:[27]

- Map out your regular routes and favorite destinations. Then use PlugShare, Blink, Chargepoint, EVGO or another charger location tool to see which charging networks are along the way. Be prepared to use any of them. This implies that you join a number of PCNs—usually at a minimal fee or no fee at all. Many networks offer a specialized Mobile app that makes on-the-road use easy and efficient.

- ChargePoint is the biggest charging network, so it's a must for nearly all Model 3 drivers.

- Other PCN options in different parts of the country (United States) are Aerovironment (Pacific Northwest) for its AV Subscription Network and SemaConnect (East Coast) as the best backup to ChargePoint.

- There are about 2,000 charging stations, mostly free, not associated with any of the networks listed below. Use PlugShare or other tools to find these chargers.

For some Model 3 owners who do not have access to a PCI, the use of a PCN may be your best charging option on a regular basis. In areas of the country with high penetrations of EVs (e.g., the San Francisco bay area, Los

27. Berman, B., "The Ultimate Guide to Electric Car ChargingNetworks, November 25, 2014, available at: http://www.plugincars.com/ultimate-guide-electric-car-charging-networks-126530.html

Angeles, Seattle, Portland and Denver, to name a few), there is growing political pressure to build out an even more robust public charging network. In many European countries this is already happening.

In some cases, municipalities are partnering with electric utilities and local businesses to build the appropriate public infrastructure. In fact, the huge popularity of the Model 3, long before the car has even been released for sale, and the impending roll-out of the GM Chevy Bolt are forcing at least some municipalities to face a future that considers public charging infrastructure for a wide array of BEVs. Here's a sample of that future provided by Leah Parks and published at Evannex's blog:[28]

> If we could step into an EV-ready community, let's say in 2018, what would we want our communities to look like?  In the mind's eye of anyone dreaming about a better electric future there would be an infrastructure to both support and utilize the amazing resource that electric vehicles can be.
>
> For example, a woman named Electra would find all she needed in the day to support her brand new 2017 Tesla Model 3. She would have an awesome home energy management and vehicle-to-grid (V2G) system that would allow for charging at low prices during the night, during which she could happily fill her battery for less than $1 per gallon equivalent. Her friend Buzz, living in an apartment nearby, would also have access to a charging system in the building's garage so he wouldn't be left out. Their utility would be happy too because, it could now have folks to sell its wind energy to instead of dumping it at night. That would keep energy suppliers and environmentalists feeling good.
>
> Electra would find more than enough chargers in the massive Walmart parking lot where she works. There would be no need to fight with other EV owners over spots. The vehicle-to-business & V2G system would allow the utility and the building to use or provide energy to the car batteries.  Now both the business (producing some of its own energy from the solar panels on its roof) and the utility are happy because there is a great new resource, employee and customer car batteries for managing both electricity load and generation.

This sounds really good, but there are a few caveats to keep in mind. Many of the chargers on a PCN today and

28. Parks, L.Y., "Riding the EV Wave: Are We Ready?," EVANNEX Blog, April 21, 2016, https://evannex.com/blogs/news/116254213-riding-the-tesla-model-3-wave-are-we-ready

in 2018 will be quite slow when compared to Tesla superchargers. For example, common chargers on any one of the networks noted earlier charge at a relatively slow rate of about 24 - 30 miles of range per hour of charging. That's okay

@evannex_com **With the exception of Tesla Superchargers, PCNs are not your best option on a day-to-day basis. Better to have a PCI. #TakeCharge #KnowYourChargers**

if you're going to spend some time shopping for clothes or groceries, but it's really a non-starter if you're on your way into work.

As time passes, it's likely that more powerful chargers will be introduced within the PCN, but for now, it's very important that you create a workable PCI. More on that in the next section.

Typical Residency Variants

## Personal Charging Infrastructure (PCI)

Before we can discuss what options are available for creating a PCI, you'll have to determine what your residence will be like when you take delivery of your Model 3. Here are a few typical residency variants for Model 3 owners:

**RV1:** You own/rent/live in a house/condo with a garage

**RV2:** You own/rent/live in a condo without a garage

**RV3:** You rent in-the-small (i.e., in a 2 – 4 family house) with a driveway or in a small apartment building with parking spaces

**RV4:** Your rent in an apartment complex with multiple buildings and parking spaces

**RV5:** You rent in a large apartment building with a parking garage

**RV6:** You rent in a building that has no provision for parking, and you park on the street

Let's take a look at how to build a PCI for each of these residency variants.

> **@evannex_com Your living situation will have a very strong bearing on the kind of PCI you can create for Model 3. #ParkingIsEverything**

**RV1: You own/rent/live in a house/condo with a garage.** Obviously, you'll have to get permission to install a PCI in the garage if you're not the owner of the property, but that shouldn't be difficult because you're paying for an improvement that will add value to the property.

Your Model 3 PCI begins at your service panel—the place where electricity from the grid gets distributed to all of the circuits in your house. You'll have to hire an electrician to run a circuit from the service panel

Typical service panel

(often, but not always, located in the garage) to the place where you'll be doing the charging for the Model 3. Let's begin with that circuit.

**The Charging Circuit.** Two charging options exist for your U.S. home — 110V-20 amp or 240V-40 or 50 amp.[29] As I mentioned earlier in the book, charging from a 110V

> **@evannex_com Your charging circuit can be simple and inexpensive, or it can be complex and cost prohibitive. Find out now! #BestLaidChargingPlans**

-20 amp circuit is very inefficient and very slow. Without getting into the physics of what is happening, a 110V

---

29. If you're unsure about what volts and amps mean, read my discussion in Chapter 1.

charge wastes about 30 – 40 percent of the electricity it uses as the charge is happening.  For example, if you need 20 kWh of charge to top off your Model 3 battery, you'll need to draw 26 to 28 kWh to get it done. Worse, it will take a very long time— about 18 - 20 hours! That just isn't acceptable. Therefore, it's much better to charge from a 240V-40 amp circuit.

> @evannex_com **Using a 110V charging circuit to charge Model 3 is like trying to use a garden hose to fill a large swimming pool. #TakesTooLong #SmartChargingSavesTime**

Tesla's premium vehicles, Model S and Model X, have on-board chargers, the device you need to take electricity from the grid and feed it properly to your car's battery. However, at the time of this writing it's unclear whether Model 3, a much lower priced car, will have an on-board charger or whether it will require the installation of an external charging unit, often referred to as *Electric Vehicle Service Equipment*, (EVSE). If you need EVSE (and remember, that's still an 'if' for Model 3), the cost of the EVSE must be added to your charging circuit installation cost. How much? That varies by region and by equipment. We'll discuss the costs in Chapter 9.

> @evannex_com **We don't yet know whether Model 3 has an on-board charger or whether an EVSE is required. #GetOnBoard**

Your Model 3 will come with a charging cable that plugs into the car's charging port. The other end of the charging cable plugs into the charging circuit installed (by a licensed electrician) in your garage or to a PCN charger. If an EVSE is required for Model 3, the charging cable will plug directly into the EVSE (usually hung on your garage wall). But if Model 3 does have an on-board charger, the charging cable provided with the car plugs into a wall receptacle (plug) that is identical to the one used for the house's oven (a NEMA 14-50 receptacle). Once further Model 3 specs are made available, we'll know which approach is required.

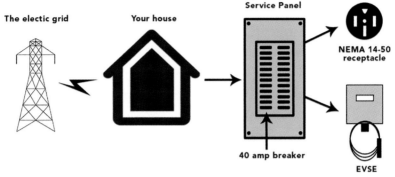

Installing the charging circuit

By the way, there are many commercially available EVSEs, ranging in price from $500 to $1000 plus installation. It's likely that Tesla will provide one specifically designed for Model 3, if that's required. In fact, the company does offer what is called a *high power wall connector* (HPWC), specifically designed for fast home charging. It's likely that a variant of the HPWC would be provided (as an option) if Model 3 does not come with an on-board charger.

**Considerations.** There are some things you have to consider as you plan your PCI installation. You will need 40 amps of capacity in your service panel—generally no problem if you live in a modern house with 200 amp service, but a potential issue if you live in an older house with only 100 amp service.

A worst-case cost scenario is if your house doesn't have adequate electrical service. If your service panel can't handle the extra load required to charge your Model 3, you're going to have to install new service and a new panel. That's expensive, so a quick check now can eliminate costly surprises later, particularly if your house is older.

In most cases, however, adding a charging circuit is fairly simple. It will require adding a new circuit and 50 amp breaker to your service panel, running appropriate cable, and making all EVSE (if required) connections. <u>This work should be done by a licensed electrician.</u>

If Model 3 requires an EVSE, choose the highest capacity charger (e.g., 30 – 40 amps) your budget can tolerate. It will provide the fastest charging and leaves room for any future needs. Be sure you place the EVSE or NEMA 14-50 receptacle near the garage door, if possible. This will allow you to charge your EV while it's parked in the driveway. There are a variety of YouTube videos that address the installation of EV charging circuits. It might be worth spending a little time watching a few.

**RV2: You own/rent/live-in a condo without a garage.** All RV1 issues apply here with the exception that your charging circuit must run to an outdoor location. This will require an outdoor electric circuit installation, substantially more linear feet of #6/4 electrical cable, and the specialized protections that must be implemented for an outdoor environment.

> **@evannex_com Outdoor installation for your charging circuit is a bit more complex, but still very do-able. #LetsChargeOutside**

In addition, if the charging location impinges on common areas or public property, approvals will have to be obtained and additional permitting will have to be acquired. It's worth looking into this now, so you have plenty of time to plan accordingly.

**RV3: You rent in-the-small (i.e., in a 2 or 4 family house).** Many of the RV2 issues apply here because it's highly likely you'll be running your circuit outdoors. In this case, the first thing that must be done is to get approval from the owner of the building. Although you are making an improvement to the owner's property, he or she may have reservations about electrical service overload. Worse, if electric service is not metered to each individual housing unit, there may be resistance to the charging circuit installation. It's important to have all the facts (e.g., costs, permitting, electric demand) before you meet with the owner and to prepare reasonable arguments to parry his or her objections, if any.

**RV4: You rent in an apartment complex with multiple buildings and parking spaces.** All RV3 issues apply here with the exception that your charging circuit must run to a parking lot, over common areas. Approval can and often will be time-consuming and difficult, and installation could be expensive, unless you can get the complex's management to foot the bill for the public good.

Among the arguments you can make in an effort to get property management to foot the bill are the obvious "green" arguments, but the owners of most apartment complexes look for a value proposition when they make an investment. Try this:

1. Collect all of the data you can find for EV ownership in your region, especially among the demographic that rents in your complex.

2. Check to determine whether your municipality or state offers incentives (e.g., grants, tax breaks) for large building owners who install EV charging equipment. If this is the case, be sure to get the details.

3. Present this data to show the owners that there is a substantial subset of potential renters who might be enticed to rent in a complex that offers BEV charging capability and that their costs can be defrayed by government grants or tax benefits.

4. Note that rental complexes that offer a "charging amenity" will be looked upon favorably by future renters with EVs and that (see step 1) the number of EV owners is growing.

5. Note further that a fee can be levied for the use of the chargers, thereby allowing the owners to recoup their investment over time.

6. Contact Tesla Motors, or, visit your local Tesla store or service center. They may be able to provide specific guidance that can "smooth" the way for you to be able to set up your PCI.

7. Visit PluginAmerica.org, the website of a U.S.-based electric vehicle advocacy organization. This site offers useful guidance for encouraging the installation of chargers in public spaces. Recently they offered a Webinar entitled "Tips on EV charging for apartment, condo and mobile home residents."

This approach is by no means foolproof and a positive result cannot be guaranteed, but if you like where you live, but really want a Model 3, it's worth pitching the need for chargers to the complex's management. And it's smart to begin *now*.

**RV5: You rent in a large apartment building with a parking garage.** Many of the RV4 issues apply, including the discussion of selling the property owners on the need to foot the bill.

**RV6: You rent in a building that has no provision for parking, and you park on the street.** This one is difficult. You may need a

> **@evannex_com If you have to park on the street, the PCI for your Model 3 could present challenges. #Sellingtheidea #RepresentEVs**

political solution, and that's never easy and rarely quick. If you are an activist, approach your local representative(s) and present data that indicates the growth of EV ownership in your locale. Do some research to determine state incentives for charger installation and also federal grants available to municipalities that are proactive. The key is this: convince your local political leadership that: (1) low cost BEVs are the future; (2) that demand for public charging will increase substantially; (3) that state and federal grants may be available (better to research this and have hard facts at your disposal); (4) that your

Street-level charging

public electric utility may have an interest in subsidizing costs; (5) that proactive policy and action are needed *now*.

On the public policy front, Leah Parks[30] comments:

The electric utilities will most certainly need to prepare and partner with businesses and governments. A recent article31 on the Pecan Street experiment in Austin, Texas demonstrates how, although a charging network is completely doable, analysis is necessary to evaluate how the grid and substations will handle the increased load. Incentives, time-of-use (TOU) programs, V2G, and smart meters will become more important as the utility strives to shift load and use car batteries for balancing during the day. This, however, brings up other issues. If car owners give utilities the right to have access to the auto's batteries, will the car manufacturers give warranties on the batteries? The good news is that justification for investing in an EV infrastructure should be easier now and a no-brainer, particularly in the most "EV Friendly" regions.

Businesses will also want to begin thinking about EV expansion implications. Investment in charging may be incentivized or even required soon. Analysis of prospects to partner with utilities for V2G and Vehicle-to-Building options will most certainly be explored in more detail. There is also new opportunity for companies developing software and the internet of things (IoT) and burgeoning charging companies as well.

30. Parks, L.Y., "Riding the EV Wave: Are We Ready?," Evannex Blog, April 21, 2016, available at: http://evannex.com/blogs/news/116254213-riding-the-tesla-model-3-wave-are-we-ready

But what if none of these suggestions work for your residential situation (RV3 – RV6). Your best option is to convince your employer to install chargers at your workplace. The approach here is similar to the strategy suggested for RV4 through RV6, but the focus must change subtly. In this case, an economic argument is important, but for larger companies, a public relations argument might be even more important. Most large companies want to be perceived as "environmentally conscious," in fact, many tout that in their public relations literature. If you put together a proposal that presents the data you've collected from RV4 and RV5 and the quasi-public policy issues raised in RV6, and the PR issues that will hit the right notes for your employer's management team, you just might have a winner.

As I mentioned earlier, it may be worthwhile to contact Tesla Motors for assistance/guidance with all of this. They might be able to help. In addition, Plug-in America (PluginAmerica.org) may also be able to provide further assistance.

31. Zurschmeide, J., "As More EVs Plug In, Can Our Power grid step UP?, Digital Trends, Nov 15, 2015, available ay: http://www.digitaltrends.com/cars/how-power-companies-plan-to-meet-electric-vehicle-charging-needs/

# CHAPTER SIX
## MODEL 3 PERFORMANCE

Tesla has street cred. In thousands of drag racing videos, many of which have gone viral, the Tesla Model S and Tesla Model X are shown smoking high-performance ICE cars that in theory should <u>not</u> have been trounced by a 5,000+ pound premium four-door sedan and/or a large SUV. And for that reason, gear-heads, automotive writers, muscle car fanatics, and car lovers in general have jettisoned their skepticism and (grudgingly) shown Tesla cars much respect.

Even the base Model 3 offers a very respectable 6-second time for 0 to 60 mph, and if my test ride is any indication, handling and general driving performance will be excellent. Other versions of Model 3 will have performance that, in time, just might rival its older siblings.

How can Model 3 exhibit such awesome performance? It's all about a torque curve that is inherent in every electric motor and the car's low center of gravity. I promise not to get too technical (at least not much), but it is important for you to understand why Model 3 performs the way it does, if for no other reason than it will help you answer the questions that will come from your friends when they hop in the car and take their first test ride.

**High Expectations**

**High Performance**

**High Enjoyment**

There's a phenomenon, documented in YouTube videos and across the Tesla forums, that occurs when someone takes their first ride in a Tesla Model S or X. I suspect the exact same phenomenon will occur for Model 3. It called the "Tesla smile," and it's the involuntary

Tesla Model s in a drag race at Palm Beach International Raceway.
(Model S smoked the lime green Dodge Hellcat)

response to a combination of awesome acceleration coupled with near silence from the car. Sometimes a first time passenger might gasp, or issue a friendly expletive, or say "Whoa!" Sometimes not. But the passenger will always smile. Let's try to understand why that happens.

## BEV Architecture

In order to better understand Model 3 performance, let's spend a little time discussing BEV "architecture"—the components that make up Model 3 and the manner in which those components work together to provide a high performance automobile. We'll try to keep our discussion simple, just enough so you understand how Model 3 works.

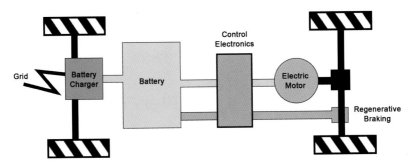

Basic architectural schematic for a BEV

This figure provides a very basic architectural diagram for a rear wheel drive BEV. Each of the components shown is integral to the operation and performance of Model 3, so it's worth understanding them.

First, the big picture: Looking at the figure from left to right, electricity from the grid is conditioned by a *charger* (in orange) that may be part of the vehicle or a separate component.[32] The charger passes electricity to the battery (in yellow). Energy stored in the battery is passed through *control electronics* (in grey) that moderate the energy flow and pass it to an electric motor (in blue). Regenerative braking (in green) translates kinetic energy of the car's forward motion into electricity and returns energy to the battery.

**The Grid and Battery Charger.** As you learned earlier in this book, the energy required to recharge your Model 3 battery comes from the electric grid.

> @evannex_com **To move electricity from the grid to the car, it has to pass through a charger. #GetOnBoard**

Each year the grid gets cleaner as coal-fired power plants are cleaned up or taken off-line and alternative energy solutions become increasingly viable. But the current coming from the grid must pass through a battery charger so that it can properly charge the Model 3 battery.

It's unclear whether a charger will be on-board and offered as part of the base Model 3 or whether you'll need an external battery charger (purchased separately) as part of your personal charging infrastructure (PCI). Regardless, the charger is as much a part of the BEV architecture as any other component.

**The Battery.** Earlier in this book, I discussed the Model 3 battery. To summarize: the bigger and better the battery,

> @evannex_com **How many kWh are enough? How much range do you need? #HighCapacityBatteries #KnowYourBatteries**

the better the BEV – the better the car's performance, the longer its range, and the more utility it offers to the owner.

32. As I mentioned earlier in the book, we don't yet know which it will be for Model 3.

But what do I mean by "bigger" and "better" ?

- 'Bigger' doesn't refer to the physical size of the battery, but rather to its storage capacity measured in kilowatt-hours.

- 'Better' refers to the battery's ability to recharge quickly as measured in hours and minutes.

Model 3 will have battery capacity and recharge times that are more than sufficient to make it competitive with ICE vehicles.

**The Electric Motor (and Torque).** The physics of an electric motor is a bit beyond the scope of this book. But a few basics are important. Coils of copper wire run through

**@evannex_com An electric motor is an example of the saying, "simplicity is excellence." #ElectricMotorsRule**

a stack of thin steel plates and form a stator . The rotor is a steel shaft with copper bars running through it. It rotates, and ultimately, turns the wheels of Model 3.

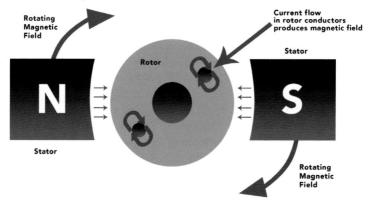

Schematic of an electric motor

But what makes the rotor rotate? The flow of alternating current into the copper windings of the stator creates a magnetic field. Alternating current causes the field to vary between N and S, appearing to move in a circular path. The rotor "chases" the magnetic field and rotates as a consequence.

Of course, there's a bit more to it, but that should give you the general idea. By the way, do you know who held many of the early patents on the electric motor? Nikola Tesla, the world-renowned scientist after whom Tesla Motors is named.

A powerful electric motor creates a substantial magnetic field, and it's the field that causes the rotor to turn. The turning force generated by the rotor—the thing that drives the wheels of Model 3— is called *torque*. Unlike an ICE, an electric motor provides instant torque (power) and variable speed (that's why Model 3 does not have a transmission—there's just no need for one). And therein lies the reason for the head-snapping quickness of Model 3.

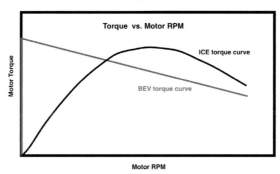

Torque curves for BEV and ICE Vehicles

The preceding figure shows the torque curve for a BEV vs. the torque curve for an ICE car. You'll note that maximum torque for a BEV occurs at zero miles per hour! That means that in the millisecond following your foot stomping on the accelerator, maximum torque is being delivered to your drive wheels. If traction control didn't exist, your tires would have trouble gripping the road and spin in place. Luckily, the traction control system (part of overall control electronics) moderates the torque so that you get only as much power as your tires can tolerate.

> @evannex_com **Loosening a stuck bolt with a wrench requires torque. #TorqueItOut**

Meanwhile torque must ramp up for an ICE vehicle. When an ICE motor is running (at idle) at low rpms, torque is very low. When a driver hits the gas, torque ramps up, but it takes a short, but still meaningful, period of time for significant power to feed to the drive wheels. So quickness is really a battle of torque curves, and Model 3 wins that one every time!

## Control Electronics

The US Department of Energy describes the control electronics for an EV in the following manner: "The electric vehicle controller is the electronics package that operates between the batteries and the motor to control the electric vehicle's speed and acceleration, much like a carburetor does in an older gasoline-powered vehicle."

> @evannex_com **Control electronics combines hardware and software to control all aspects of the Model 3 architecture. #Computeron4Wheels**

The control electronics perform the following functions:

- transforms DC current from the battery into AC (for AC motors) and regulates the energy flow from the battery
- reverses the motor rotation (so the vehicle can go in reverse)
- converts the motor into a generator so that the kinetic energy can be used to recharge the battery during regenerative braking

Model 3 will have a sophisticated suite of control electronics hardware and software that performs the functions noted above and also optimizes battery usage so that the greatest possible range is achieved for any given speed. For a dual motor, all wheel drive (AWD) version of Model 3, the control electronics hardware and software distributes power to the front and rear motors to perform all functions noted previously.

## Regenerative Braking

Earlier in this book, we talked briefly about *regenerative braking* (regen) and about how it converts the kinetic energy of Model 3 into energy that recharges the car's battery. To get geeky for a moment, kinetic energy is a function of Model 3's mass and its velocity squared. The mass of any car is huge, and when Model 3 is going fast, its kinetic energy goes up as the square of the velocity. That means there's a lot of KE for regen to capture.

That's why the brake pads in any vehicle become very, very hot as you brake— kinetic energy of the car is dissipated as heat. In a BEV the kinetic energy is partially recaptured using regen.

The transformation is really quite simple. When you remove your foot from the accelerator, the control electronics sense this action and the electric motor is switched and becomes a generator that produces current that is sent back to the battery, recharging it.

But be careful with your assumptions here. Not all of the kinetic energy is converted into current, because there are losses in the conversion. If there were

> **@evannex_com** **Do you know why there will be very little brake dust on Model 3 wheels? #Regen**

no losses, all BEVs would be perpetual motion machines— and that's impossible. But a BEV does capture as much as 40 – 50 percent of the car's kinetic energy and reuses it, recharging the battery as you travel. And that's pretty cool.

## Vehicle Performance

Wikipedia[33] lists 24 vehicle performance metrics, all important and measurable, but many (as yet) unknown for Model 3. For our purposes, we'll consider a smaller number of quantitative and qualitative indicators of performance:

---

33. Wikipedia, "Vehicular Metrics," available at https://en.wikipedia.org/wiki/Vehicular_metrics

**Quickness.** Most automobile buffs love quickness, the head snapping acceleration that

occurs when you have a high performance car. But quickness alone is only half the story. Even better is smooth, but extremely rapid acceleration—no jerks or hesitation, no unevenness, no lag between the time you hit the accelerator and the time the car begins to move forward.

Because it is a BEV, Model 3 provides smooth acceleration and because it has a large battery and a capable electric motor, it offers rather surprising quickness.

In the first part of this chapter, you learned that quickness is a result of an electric motor's torque curve—power is delivered to the drive wheels almost instantaneously.

Performance

**Motor horsepower.** You've heard the term "horsepower" your entire adult life, but do you know what it actually means? One horsepower represents the work required to move 550 pounds one foot in one second. That really doesn't tell you much, except that the higher the motor horsepower the more work it can do.

In reality, horsepower is a function of the torque delivered by a motor. A car is placed on a dynamometer—a device that is used to measure torque. Horsepower is computed once torque is known. HowStuffWorks.com[34] describes how this is done:

> Horsepower is determined from torque because torque is easier to measure. Torque is defined specifically as a rotating force that may or may not result in motion. It's measured as the amount of force multiplied by the length of the lever through which it acts. For example, if you use a one-foot-long wrench to apply 10 pounds of force to a bolt head, you're generating 10-pound-feet of torque.

34. Baxter, E., What's the difference between horsepower and torque," http://auto.howstuffworks.com/difference-between-torque-and-horsepower.htm

Torque, as mentioned above, can be generated without moving an object. However, when it does move an object, it then becomes "work," and this is what most people think of when they think of torque (usually in terms of towing). The more torque produced by an engine, the more work potential it has.

The actual calculation for horsepower (HP) goes like this:

**HP = (torque x motor rpm) / 5252**

Tesla has not yet announced the HP that will be available for the base Model 3 or for the higher performance version(s), but you can rest assured that even for the base version of the car, it will be sufficient to make Model 3 quick.

Model 3 cornering (Photo © Kyle Field, 2016, courtesy of Clean Technica)

## Handling

Some people believe that all cars handle well enough, and that a discussion of handling is just esoteric car stuff. However, vehicle handling is important, not only if you've decided to try a slalom course, but if you encounter a driving emergency (e.g., someone suddenly cuts you off), or you are about to miss a turn you really do have to take. Your car does have to handle well in those situations. But what does handling really mean? Aaron Gold[35] provides a layperson's definition:

35. Gold, A., "All About Handling," Vroomgirls.com, available at: http://www.vroomgirls.com/all-about-handling/

Handling generally refers to how a car responds when it turns. A car with better handling can go around corners or turns at higher speeds and is less likely to lose control in a sudden panic swerve. How well a car handles is largely a function of the car's suspension — the bits and pieces that attach the wheels to the car and allow them to move up and down — but the steering and tires as well as the vehicle's weight also play major roles.

A car with poor handling tends to roll (tilt) as it goes around curve; it tends to experience nose dive when you hit the brakes hard, and it tends to slide (drift) if you take a corner at too high a speed.

Yet, we don't yet know a lot about the specifics of the Model 3 suspension, the production tires that it will **@evannex_com Handling matters—especially when you drive into a curve at high speed! #Model3Performs** have, or the final vehicle weight. So how can I claim that Model 3 will have good handling? First, its older siblings, Model S and Model X have excellent handling, and both are archetypes for Model 3. Second, Model 3 has a very low center of gravity due to its skateboard design—a big and heavy battery sits very low on the chassis. The lower the CG (center of gravity), the less roll you'll experience when cornering.

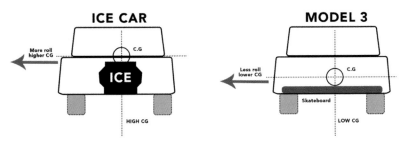

Center of Gravity (C.G.) for a typical ICE car and Model 3

Referring to the figure, you'll note that a high CG creates a larger tipping "moment" (an obscure engineering term) than a car with a lower CG. Think of it this way—it's much easier to push over a tall thin object that weighs the same and has the same base dimensions as a short object.

The reason is that the CG is lower for the short object. Therefore, Model 3 rolls less because its CG is so low.

In addition, because the battery is a large rectangular object with a relatively homogeneous structure sitting under Model 3, it distributes weight more evenly across all four wheels, resulting in better cornering stability and traction. Also, because the CG is close to the center of the vehicle (i.e., the center of a rectangle with the wheels at each corner), Model 3 can change direction in a nimble fashion.

If you have additional interest in handling, spend a few minutes reading through the Wikipedia discussion.[36] You'll learn a lot of new terminology and be better prepared for vehicle reviews of Model 3 as the production date nears.

36. Wikipedia, Automobile handling, available at: https://en.wikipedia.org/wiki/Automobile_handling

# CHAPTER SEVEN
## MODEL 3 AS AN AUTONOMOUS VEHICLE

I'm old school. I love to drive, and having a car drive for me seems … well… slightly off. But on the other hand, most of the driving I do (and I suspect most of the driving you do) is tedious—a daily commute, the weekly or monthly trip on the interstate to visit family, long road trips covering hundreds of miles on boring freeways. It would really be nice to turn the driving task over to a driver that would never get tired, never daydream, and never look at a the phone when it indicated an incoming call, email, or text. That driver just might be Model 3.

Think about it for just a moment. Driving has been a 'hands-busy, eyes-busy' activity for over a century. When you drive you can talk or listen, but you absolutely should not do anything that requires looking away from the road or taking your hands off the steering wheel. That's why texting while driving is illegal, dangerous, and a very bad idea. Wouldn't it be nice if you could do something productive or entertaining during a tedious or long drive? You could put the finishing touches on a Powerpoint presentation for a new client; create a report that you've been putting off, catch

**Less**
Drive Focus
**Less**
Drive Stress
**More**
Overall Safety

up on email, use social media with impunity, even watch a video. All the while, your car does the driving for you – safely.

That's the thinking behind the push for autonomous driving, and Elon Musk has already implied that all Model 3s will have a sensor suite that will support it. The big question is: How much autonomy will be offered? Today, Tesla vehicles (Model S and X) are equipped with "autopilot" functionality and can drive autonomously on interstates, can park themselves, and can be summoned from a remote location. It's extremely likely that those capabilities and more will be available for Model 3 as an extra cost option.

In this chapter, I'll explain current autonomous driving tech with the intent of preparing you for a decision on what options you might select as part of an autonomous Model 3.

## Autonomous Driving

Few would debate that autonomous driving is the future, and Model 3 may be the first relatively low cost vehicle to offer state-of-the-art autonomous driving features. In fact, it's likely that Model 3 will force big auto to offer autonomous driving functions in ICE vehicles at the same price point as Model 3. The big question, I suppose, is who will do the best job of it? In addition, tech companies like Apple and Google are not sitting idly by. It's also likely that they will offer cars and/or software and hardware that just might make autonomous driving ubiquitous within a decade or less.

> @evannex_com **Model 3 will offer autonomous driving features. The question is how much, how soon? #AutoPilotIsReal #LookMaNoHands**

Slash Gear[37] predicts: "Tesla's going to leapfrog rivals with Model 3 Autopilot ... Tesla's Model 3 could take pole position in a new breed of near-autonomous vehicles."

But let's not get ahead of ourselves. First, you should understand the levels of "autonomous driving," then the state of current tech, and finally, just what the Model 3 might offer.

37. http://www.slashgear.com/teslas-going-to-leapfrog-rivals-with-model-3-autopilot-08435480/

# Levels of Autonomous Driving

The U.S. Department of Transportation (USDoT) is rightly concerned about the safety and reliability of autonomous vehicles. To help better understand the various levels of autonomy that automobile manufacturers might offer, the USDoT defines five levels:[38]

- **No-Automation (Level 0):** The driver is in complete and sole control of the primary vehicle controls – brake, steering, throttle, and motive power – at all times.

- **Function-specific Automation (Level 1):** Automation at this level involves one or more specific control functions. Examples include electronic stability control or pre-charged brakes, where the vehicle automatically assists with braking to enable the driver to regain control of the vehicle or stop faster than possible by acting alone.

- **Combined Function Automation (Level 2):** This level involves automation of at least two primary control functions designed to work in unison to relieve the driver of control of those functions. An example of combined functions enabling a Level 2 system is adaptive cruise control in combination with lane centering.

- **Limited Self-Driving Automation (Level 3):** Vehicles at this level of automation enable the driver to cede full control of all safety-critical functions under certain traffic or environmental conditions and in those conditions to rely heavily on the vehicle to monitor for changes in those conditions requiring transition back to driver control. The driver is expected to be available for occasional control, but with sufficiently comfortable transition time. The Google car is an example of limited self-driving automation.

36. U.S. DoT, Policy on Automated vehicle development, May,2013, available at: http://www.nhtsa.gov/About+NHTSA/Press+Releases/U.S.+Department+of+Transportation+Releases+Policy+on+Automated+Vehicle+Development

- **Full Self-Driving Automation (Level 4):** The vehicle is designed to perform all safety-critical driving functions and monitor roadway conditions for an entire trip. Such a design anticipates that the driver will provide destination or navigation input, but is not expected to be available for control at any time during the trip. This includes both occupied and unoccupied vehicles.

At the moment, Tesla "autopilot" is close to or at USDoT's Level 3. The real question is how far the company will progress over the next few years and whether Model 3 will have the tech to achieve Level 4.

## Current Tech

Fully autonomous driving has become the holy grail for a number of important tech companies. Google, one of the major players in the field, uses a system called LIDAR (light detection and ranging) to provide the necessary input to its suite of autonomous driving sensors and software. In essence, LIDAR fires pulses of laser light in all directions, times their echoes, and creates a very precise (accurate to less than an inch) three-dimensional map of everything that surrounds the car—e.g., other vehicles, stationary objects, pedestrians, curbs, signs. LIDAR works and works well, but it requires expensive hardware and software. Currently, a full LIDAR implementation costs tens of thousand of dollars, adding significant manufacturing costs for a car. Less costly LIDAR systems are under development, but they still are projected to cost more than $5,000 per car at the manufactured level.

Apple is also purportedly working on autonomous driving tech, but as always, it has been very secretive about its efforts. No one outside the company knows the technology specifics of Apple's approach.

## The Tesla Approach

As you probably know, Tesla CEO Elon Musk is not averse to breaking with convention and taking risks. He rejected the LIDAR approach as too expensive and decided to go another way. Levi Tillemann and Colin McCormick[39] describe the approach:

> [Musk] believed that Tesla could get the same results with a cheaper suite of sensors. Musk first revealed that Tesla was considering adding autonomous-driving features in 2013. Tesla's ultimate strategy was to bypass lidar with a combination of simple cameras, radar (which uses radio waves to estimate distances to objects that are farther away), and ultrasound (which uses sound waves to estimate the distance to objects in the immediate vicinity). The cameras, which aren't much different from the ones used in smartphones, produce a video stream that is then analyzed by algorithms trained to recognize objects. Tesla's key partner for the camera system is Mobileye, an Israeli computer-vision company which claims that its software can detect vehicles up to two hundred and thirty feet away using a single standard-resolution camera—all while adding only a thousand dollars to the price of a car.

But here's the thing. Tesla has something that other car companies don't—the ability to monitor and track its cars (with owner permission, of course) in real-time via the Internet. That means that the company can gather big data on its cars. And when Tesla Motors allowed owners to engage its already built-in, but limited "autopilot" system,[40] the company was able to conduct a massive 'beta test' of the technology. Again, from Tillemann and McCormick:

> Autopilot also gave Tesla access to tens of thousands of "expert trainers," as Musk called them. When these de-facto test drivers overrode the system, Tesla's sensors and learning algorithms took special note. The company has used its growing data set to continually improve the autonomous-driving experience for Tesla's entire fleet. By late 2015, Tesla was gathering about a million miles' worth of driving data every day.

A million miles of real world data every day! This gives Tesla an enormous competitive advantage. Rather than relying on a small fleet of test vehicles (e.g., Google has about 80 LIDAR equipped test vehicles on the road),

39. Tillemann, L and C. McCormick, "Will the Tesla Model 3 be the first truly self-driving car?, The New Yorker, April, 16, 2016, available at: http://www.newyorker.com/business/currency/will-the-tesla-model-3-be-the-first-truly-self-driving-car

Tesla has tens of thousands of cars, collecting data that can be used to refine and improve its autonomous driving hardware and software.

Tesla is betting that a system of relatively low cost sensors, coupled with very sophisticated image recognition and control software, will allow the Model 3 to achieve USDoT Level 3 autonomous capabilities by the time it is released for sale. At some point further down the line, the same Model 3 you buy might receive an over-the-air update and rise to USDoT Level 4.

Model 3 is still a way off, and there's really no way we can predict how far autonomous driving capabilities will advance between now and the time the car is released. But the current autopilot capabilities of the Tesla Model S and Model X do provide a good baseline for what you'll see when you're asked to configure your car. It may be that Model 3 will offer substantially more and different autonomous driving capabilities—a near certainty in the years following production release. But at the beginning, autopilot is probably what you'll get—and autopilot is pretty significant. Let's take a look at "autopilot" features currently available for Model S and Model X.

Image used with the permission of Tesla Motors.

**Autosteer.** A combination of "traffic aware cruise control," a front facing camera, and side sensors, keeps the Model S

---

40. This was accomplished via an over-the-air (OTA) software update, beaned to each Model S that had the sensor suite for autonomous driving.

(and Model X) in its current lane and will moderate vehicle speed so that the Model S or X flows with traffic. The driver does not need to manipulate the steering wheel or to keep his or her foot on the accelerator or brake. However, Tesla notes that drivers must "remain engaged and aware when Autosteer is enabled. Drivers must keep their hands on the steering wheel."

**Auto lane change.** Many accidents occur when a driver changes lanes. The reason is that it's difficult to see cars off the rear driver side or passenger side bumper—the infamous 'blind spot.' Tesla's autopilot allows safe lane changes by monitoring the blind spot and following traffic. The human driver simply pushes the turn signal stalk and the Model S or X will change lanes when it is safe to do, moderating speed and steering accordingly.

Image used with permission of Tesla Motors

**Emergency Steering and Side Collision Warning.** The existing sensor suite on Model S and X can accurately detect objects, including other cars, that are near the vehicle. When this happens, "fluid lines" (see figure) will radiate from the vehicle image on the dash display to warn the driver.

Image used with permission of Tesla Motors

**Autopark.** Like many conventional vehicles, Model S and X can autopark. When driving at low speed in an urban setting, the Model S or X can sense an open parking space and display a "P" on the instrument

Image used with permission of Tesla Motors

panel. An autopark guide will appear on the touchscreen along with the rear camera display. Once initiated, the vehicle will perform the parallel parking maneuver without human intervention.

**Summon.** Today, this feature is fairly rudimentary (how quickly we all become blasé about sophisticated automation), but soon, *summon* will become a really important autonomous driving feature. Currently, *summon* allows Model S or Model X to drive itself autonomously and park in your garage, or to exit from your garage. Soon, however, *summon* will allow the owner to summon the car from a distance using the Tesla smartphone app. The car will move from a public parking space (e.g., at a mall or other business) and pick you up. Think about the benefits when there is inclement weather!

There is every reason to believe that Model 3 will have all of the autonomous driving features that are currently available for Model S or X. Undoubtedly, these features will be part of an extra cost option, but I believe that the benefit justifies the cost for many Model 3 owners.

By the time Model 3 is released, it's very likely that new sensors, new software and new and exciting functionality will be available for autonomous driving. Model 3 will likely offer all of those new features.

# CHAPTER EIGHT
## WHEN CAN I EXPECT MY MODEL 3 TO BE DELIVERED?

I ordered my "Signature" Tesla Model S in 2011, long before production versions of the car would be available. At that time, early adopters of the Tesla Model S formed a small and enthusiastic community. Many of us communicated daily on the Tesla forums. We argued and speculated about the car's features, its performance, and its design successes and fails (as we saw them). But above all, we began to guess the date when the Model S would leave the factory in Fremont, California and be delivered into our hands. Does any of that sound familiar? It should, because hundreds of thousands of people who are on the Model 3 reservation list are now doing the same thing.

But back to the Model S for a moment. As those of us on that reservation list tried to bide our time, months passed and speculation mounted about the delivery date. Rumored delivery dates were common. First, in late 2011, then in early 2012, then later in Spring, 2012. Finally, the very first cars came off the line, and in June 2012, the Model S hit the streets in limited numbers.

### Tesla Time

Our company, EVANNEX, sells aftermarket accessories for Model S, Model X, and soon, for Model 3. We have enormous respect for Tesla Motors, for their engineering prowess, their manufacturing abilities, and their forward thinking, risk-tolerant leadership. We were the first outside company in what I call the Tesla "ecosystem," and we've had an opportunity to observe the company for quite some time.

One thing we've noticed is that Tesla Motors operates on "Tesla time." Quite frequently, the infectious optimism that pervades the company causes its leadership to announce release dates for products that are ... well ... aggressive. Often, Tesla will miss those dates—sometimes by a little, and sometimes by a lot.

> @evannex_com **Tesla operates on its own clock. #TeslaTime**

The company has been criticized for this by the financial and automotive media, and by more than a few anxious customers who *really, really* want their cars. But 'Tesla time' is real, and it has to be taken into account whenever projections for delivery dates are made. Then again, past performance isn't necessarily an indication of future results. It may be that Tesla Motors, recognizing the historic importance of a relatively low cost BEV on both its business and the future of electric cars, may move heaven and earth[41] to get Model 3 delivered on time, with early deliveries beginning in late 2017.

Imagine—Your Model 3 leaving the factory
(Photo © Kyle Field, 2016, courtesy of Clean Technica)

41. In the May, 2016 earning call, Elon Musk said, "Tesla is gonna be hell-bent on becoming the best manufacturer on Earth."

For the remainder of this chapter, I use past history and current projections from Tesla itself to make a series of educated guesses about the delivery ramp for Model 3, the production rates that can be derived from the delivery ramp, and from all of that, propose an approach that will enable you to determine when you can expect to get your Model 3. Obviously, all of this is *speculation*. No one (probably not even Tesla Motors) can make these projections with any degree of assurance at this time. But nonetheless, it's fun to try, and it will provide you with a reality check for when you might get Model 3 delivered to your door.

## Past Production History

In order to get a better understanding of production rates and the delivery ramp for Model 3, it might be instructive to examine some of Tesla's production rate numbers for Model S. But there are a few caveats:

- Model S and Model 3 are different vehicles. Model S is a premium vehicle that was not engineered for high volume production. Model 3 is a mass-market vehicle designed and engineered for higher production rates.

- Tesla was a relative neophyte when Model S production began. It has undoubtedly learned much from Model S production that can help it improve Model 3 production dramatically.

- Model S production rates were dictated by customer demand and therefore are tied to Model S quarterly orders received by Tesla. The order flow for Model 3 will be many multiples of Model S order flow, thereby driving production significantly.

Yet, even with these important differences, an examination of Model S data can serve to ground expectations for early Model 3 production and delivery.

In the third quarter of 2013, the first full quarter of production for Model S, Tesla delivered 5,500 vehicles for a weekly average production rate of 423 cars. The following graph, derived from information published in Tesla Quarterly reports, provides an indication of cars produced (in blue) and weekly average production rate (in red) for each quarter that followed to the time at which this is being written.

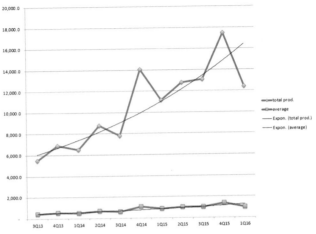

Tesla Model S production data 3Q13 to 1Q16

Referring to the graph, quarterly production since 2013 follows the black trend line that passes through the points on the blue graph. Over 11 quarters, production has increased from 5,500 cars per quarter to around 16,000 cars per quarter. Similarly, a black trend line through points on the red curve indicates that average weekly production rate has increased from approximately 420 cars per week to around 1,300 cars per week.

But the real question is whether these data have any bearing whatsoever on Model 3 production numbers.

## Tesla's Latest Production Projections

In their first quarter, 2016 shareholder report, Tesla management writes:

We are on track to achieve volume Model 3 production and deliveries in late 2017. Of course, in order to meet that timeframe, we will be holding both ourselves and our suppliers accountable to be ready for volume production in advance of that timing. Additionally, given the demand for Model 3, we have decided to advance our 500,000 total unit build plan (combined for Model S, Model X, and Model 3) to 2018, two years earlier than previously planned. Increasing production five fold over the next two years will be challenging and will likely require some additional capital, but this is our goal and we will be working hard to achieve it. We remain on plan to make the first cells at the Gigafactory in Q4 2016, and we are adjusting our plans there to accommodate our revised build plan.

The key phrases when considering estimates of delivery ramp and production are:

- "We are on track to achieve volume Model 3 production and deliveries in late 2017", and

- "...we have decided to advance our 500,000 total unit build plan (combined for Model S, Model X, and Model 3) to 2018"

In the earnings call on May 4, 2016, Elon Musk expanded on these claims by stating that his target was a start to Model 3 production on July 1, 2017, although later he said that realistically, a July 1st start would be "impossible." But he went on to argue that the delivery ramp for Model 3 would be very steep in 2017 and that "between 100,000 and 200,000 cars would be delivered by year end. These are very bold statements indeed, and I will consider them as I discuss the delivery ramp, production rates and a method for estimating delivery of your Model 3.

## The Delivery Ramp

The *delivery ramp* for Model 3 is a measure of how quickly Tesla Motors will increase production over a period of many months once Model 3 deliveries begin. The delivery ramp takes the shape of an S-curve illustrated in the following graphical representation. During the first months of production, delivery growth will be quite low, but once kinks are worked out, it will accelerate rapidly. Then it will moderate but continue to grow as additional efficiencies are found to improve the production process.

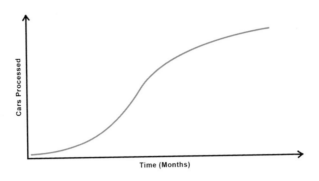

Typical delivery ramp for production

No matter how hard Tesla tries to maintain Elon Musk's aggressive 2017 delivery predictions for Model 3, there are a few harsh realities that must be taken into account. As I just mentioned, the production rate (cars produced per week) will ramp up slowly. This is both predictable and prudent. After all, every production line must be validated, the supply-chain must be established and verified, quality must be closely controlled, and bugs in both manufacturing tooling and the car must be worked out. During the early days of production, things will go wrong: equipment (robots, tooling, presses, transport machines, etc.) may not be right, supply chain issues may arise, a parts vendor may drop the ball—in essence, manufacturing something as complex as Model 3 is an open invitation to Murphy's law—*What can go wrong will go wrong, and at the worst possible time.* I know this sounds pessimistic, but I've had a bit of experience in manufacturing, and I can tell you that it's just being realistic.

**@evannex_com "Speculation" is just a fancy word for guessing. #Guesses**

So after what I've just said, what can you realistically expect for the delivery ramp for Model 3? That's a difficult question to answer, but I'm happy to speculate, as long as you recognize that Tesla Motors may surprise us all and ramp much more rapidly (or possibly, much more slowly) than I predict.

Where to begin?

**The NUMMI Plant.** We know that the Tesla Motors plant in Fremont, CA (often referred to as the NUMMI plant) is capable of producing 500,000 cars each year. That level of production was achieved during its heyday as a Toyota-GM (NUMMI) partnership. Tesla has completely re-outfitted the plant with state-of-the-art equipment and considerably better automation, but the maximum production rate is likely to remain at 500,000 cars per year when Model 3 is in full production.

The Fremont Plant (a.k.a. NUMMI)

Currently, the Fremont plant is forecast to produce about 85,000 vehicles (Model S and Model X) per year at the time of this writing. For 2017, it is projected to produce about 60,000 Model S and another 60,000 Model X. Those production figures are likely to remain fairly static through 2020. Therefore, assuming an upper limit of 500,000 vehicles for the factory, the available capacity for Model 3 is 380,000 vehicles each year or a maximum weekly average of 7,300 cars per week. But remember, the delivery ramp must be considered.

> @evannex_com **The "delivery ramp" is what every Model 3 reservation holder will be watching. ##TeslaTime**

**Production Rates from Other Manufacturers.** Before I make some estimates regarding the Model 3 delivery ramp and the production rate (in cars per week) that Tesla Motors might achieve during the first few years of Model

3 production, it's worth examining the production rates achieved by other automotive manufacturers in the United States.

Automobilemag.com[42] published an instructive article delineating the 15 "top-producing" car plants in the U.S. At the bottom of the list is a Ford plant (Chicago, IL) that produces an impressive average of 5,053 cars per week. In the middle of the list we find Kia Motors Plant (West Point, GA) that produces 5,430 cars per week. Near the top, Hyundai (Montgomery, AL) produces about 6,580 cars per week.

These numbers will help to ground my estimates of average weekly production rate. Every auto plant noted in the "Top-15" has been in operation for years, has been debugged, has a continuing flow of improvements, automation and the like. It is only reasonable to assume that as Tesla Motors brings its Model 3 production on-line, it will take time and refinement to achieve the levels of production evidenced by manufacturers such as Ford, Kia, and Hyundai.

**Estimating the Ramp.** Trying to estimate what the Model 3 delivery ramp might look like is pure guesswork. However, the Model S and Model X delivery ramps provide some clues, although it's fair to note that Tesla Motors is now more mature and has significantly more experience in rolling out cars from its Fremont production facility. As I mentioned earlier in this chapter, the Model 3 was designed for manufacture from the ground up (Model S and X were not). For that reason, the Model S and X delivery ramps may not be applicable for Model 3. Finally, Tesla's 1Q16 Investor's Report and Elon Musk's explanatory comments state that ""We are on track to achieve volume Model 3 production and deliveries in late 2017." The implication of this is that early production might begin in 3Q17 and then accelerate into 4Q17.

42. Holmes, J., "The 15 Top-Producing American Car Plants," Automobile, July 4, 2012, available at: http://www.automobilemag.com/news/the-15-top-producing-american-car-plants-151801/

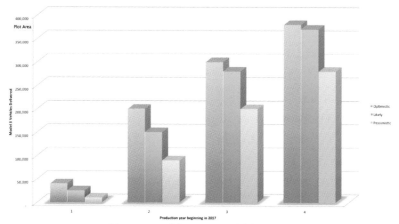

Macro view of the estimated delivery ramp

The preceding histogram is my attempt to synthesize a <u>speculative</u> macro-view (cars produced per year) of the delivery ramp under three sets of operational conditions:

- *Optimistic*—all preproduction/vehicle design work goes according to schedule, all factory requirements are implemented without any significant problems, the Tesla Gigafactory is producing batteries at a rate that is fully acceptable, all other supply chain issues are resolved to Tesla's satisfaction.

- *Likely*—minor problems occur in preproduction/vehicle design but are solved quickly, there are hiccups as the factory comes on-line but solutions and workarounds have been instantiated, the Gigafactory is humming along, and supply chain issues that do exist are resolved quickly

- *Pessimistic*—lots of things go wrong and the subsequent delays are not resolved quickly, the production rate of batteries at the Gigafactory does not meet expectations, the supply chain is a continuing challenge.

In tabular form the delivery ramp can be represented as follows:

| Year | Optimistic | Likely | Pessimistic |
|------|-----------|--------|-------------|
| 2017 | 40,000 | 25,000 | 10,000 |
| 2018 | 200,000 | 150,000 | 90,000 |
| 2019 | 300,000 | 280,000 | 200,000 |
| 2020 | 380,000 | 370,000 | 280,000 |

Estimated Model 3 Vehicles Produced and Delivered

You'll note that I have dramatically discounted Elon Musk's claim of 100,000 Model 3 deliveries in 2017.[43] Think "Tesla Time!" I estimate that Model 3 deliveries in 2017 will number in the 25,000 vehicle range, if Tesla can achieve the "volume production" it projects for "late 2017." Given the company's further claims for 2018, I estimate that the ramp will increase by a factor of six to 150,000 vehicles (far below Elon's predictions, but still quite impressive). In 2019, a near doubling to 280,000 vehicles, and finally, in 2020, production at or near full capacity.

## Production Rate Projections

Past history has indicated that the delivery ramp for both Model S and Model X was relatively slow in the first year, but Tesla was still in its infancy as a manufacturer, Models S and X were not built for easy manufacturing, and production kinks still had to be worked out at the time. Tesla claims that things will be different for Model 3, but the big question is: How different?

If your eyes glaze over when you see the tables and production numbers that follow, rest assured that they'll be very helpful for estimating the delivery date of your Model 3, so they are important.

@evannex_com Although some Model 3s will be delivered in 2017, don't bet the farm that yours will be one of them, unless you stood in line on day 1. #PatienceIsAVirtue #AnAnnoyingVirtue

**2017 Deliveries.** My estimates under a *likely* set of operational conditions have Tesla Motors producing only about 25,000 Model S vehicles toward the end of 2017, substantially less than predicted by Elon Musk. Even under *optimistic* conditions, I would be surprised if Tesla produced more than 40,000 Model 3 vehicles by year-end, 2017.

43. Frankly, I think that would be an amazing achievement, given the tight timelines and difficulty of the task.

Obviously, the company could surprise us all and ramp up much more rapidly, but that has not been Tesla's *modus operandi* in the past. Part of the reason for the slow ramp-up is the need to conduct "secondary beta-tests" for the first few thousand vehicles released to the field. If significant issues are encountered during the first few months of field use, those issues are relatively easy to resolve. In addition, if the secondary beta-tests indicate that production changes are required, those changes can be made without the need to retrofit a large number of cars. Bottom line—the 25,000 Model 3s I predict for 2017 will go to selected west coast residents, Tesla Model S and X owners, and other VIPs.

Table 1 provides an estimate of production rates for 2017.

| 2017-Quarter | avg. wk. rate | cars in quarter | cumulative cars |
|---|---|---|---|
| 1Q | 0 | - | - |
| 2Q | 0 | - | - |
| 3Q | 250 | 3,250 | 3,250 |
| 4Q | 1650 | 21,450 | 24,700 |
| Production total | | 24,700 | 24,700 |
| Average rate | | 475 | |

Table 1. Estimated Weekly Average Production -2017

**2018 Production Rates.** My educated guess (and it is a guess) is that during 2018, Tesla will achieve an average production rate of approximately 2,825 cars per week, somewhere close to the *likely* set of operational conditions for the delivery ramp. This is illustrated in Table 2:

> @evannex_com **2018 will be the year of Model 3. That's when a large number of cars will hit the streets. #YearofModel3**

| 2018-Quarter | avg. wk. rate | cars in quarter | cumulative cars |
|---|---|---|---|
| 1Q | 2000 | 26,000 | 50,700 |
| 2Q | 2500 | 32,500 | 83,200 |
| 3Q | 3100 | 40,300 | 123,500 |
| 4Q | 3700 | 48,100 | 171,600 |
| Production total | | 146,900 | 171,600 |
| Average rate | | 2,825 | |

Table 2. Estimated Weekly Average Production -2018

Referring to Table 2, during 1Q18 my guess is that the production rate will average about 2,000 cars per week, with rapid acceleration of around 2,500 cars per week during 2Q18, and still more acceleration into the second half of the year for an annual weekly average of 2,825 cars per week. Although these might be viewed as pessimistic by some, note that they are, at least toward the end of 2018, almost three times Tesla's current weekly production rate for Model S.

**2019 Production Rates.** Continuing my speculation, let's consider 2019 (Table 3). Weekly production rates will accelerate in 2019 with, and remember this is speculative, an average production rate for the year of about 5,375 cars per week, yielding about 280,000 cars produced for 2019. By the end of the year, Tesla will have produced roughly 450,000 Model 3 vehicles.

| 2019-Quarter | avg. wk. rate | cars in quarter | cumulative cars |
|---|---|---|---|
| 1Q | 4200 | 54,600 | 226,200 |
| 2Q | 5000 | 65,000 | 291,200 |
| 3Q | 5800 | 75,400 | 366,600 |
| 4Q | 6500 | 84,500 | 451,100 |
| Production total | | 279,500 | 451,100 |
| Average rate | | 5,375 | |

Table 3. Estimated Weekly Average Production -2019

The average production rate that I predict is in the range of the "top producing" car plants discussed earlier in this chapter. Those rates are in the 5,000 to 6,000 cars per week range. I think it's reasonable to estimate that Tesla will achieve about 90 percent of that rate as an annual yearly average for 2019.

If demand for Model 3 is as strong as I believe it will be, it's likely that Tesla Motors will begin the construction of another manufacturing facility in either Europe or Asia to increase the

@evannex_com **Almost all reservation holders through May, 2016 will have received the Model 3s by year-end, 2019. #TheWaitsOver**

number of cars it can build per year. Elon Musk has hinted at this possibility as well. Construction of a new plant might begin in 2019, but a fully operational manufacturing plant would not come on line until 2020, at the earliest.

**2020 Production Rates.** By 2020, it is possible that the Fremont plant will reach full production capacity. Table 4 provides my best guess on weekly numbers.

| 2020-Quarter | avg. wk. rate | cars in quarter | cumulative cars |
|---|---|---|---|
| 1Q | 7000 | 91,000 | 542,100 |
| 2Q | 7200 | 93,600 | 635,700 |
| 3Q | 7200 | 93,600 | 729,300 |
| 4Q | 7200 | 93,600 | 822,900 |
| Production total | | 371,800 | 822,900 |
| Average rate | | 7,150 | |

Table 4. Estimated Weekly Average Production -2020

At this stage, the Fremont plant is at capacity, producing about 370,000 Model 3s per year. It should also be noted that it would rocket to near the top of the "top producing" list of auto plants in the U.S.

## Reservation History

Many of you stood in line for hours on March 31, 2016 to be among the first to plunk down $1,000 to reserve a Model 3. The worldwide response over the next few weeks was absolutely astonishing and jolted the automotive world. The massive reservation numbers more than validated interest in BEVs and indicated that a substantial market for the right BEV did exist.

The graph on the top of the next page illustrates the reservation history for Model 3 over the first two weeks of April, 2016.

In the next section, we'll use this reservation history along with the delivery ramp and speculative production rate numbers in Tables 1 through 4 to come up with a time window for your delivery.

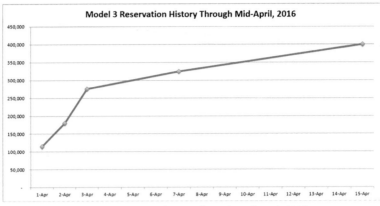

Model 3 reservation history through mid-April, 2016

## Estimating Your Model 3 Delivery Date

Before I make some broad predictions about when you might actually receive your Model 3, it's important to raise a few salient points:

First, Tesla executives have stated that very early (3Q17) Model 3 deliveries will be skewed to the West coast of United States. The reason for this is to allow Tesla to conduct what I have called "secondary beta tests" to ensure product quality and reliability in early cars delivered to the field.

Electrek.com[44] discusses the roll-out strategy by interpreting tweets offered by Elon Musk and other Tesla executives. They write:

> Also mentioned by Musk were some clarifications on the geographical roll-out. Model 3 orders will be sorted and ranked geographically, meaning you will have a reservation sequence number for your particular area, not necessarily on the entire order list. Despite the high number of orders, Musk mentions that ordering now [April 3, 2016] will make a large difference for your particular location.

After the first cars are delivered, it remains likely that the first large-scale deliveries of Model 3 will continue to occur within North America. European reservations and reservations coming from other parts of the world will likely

44. Electrk.com, "Model 3 Mega Tweetstorm," April 3, 2016, available at: http://electrek.co/2016/04/03/model-3-tweetstorm-tons-of-new-info-on-production-ramp-dashboard-trunk-and-more-updating/

be delayed, possibly for a significant period of time. This has been Tesla's approach for both Model S and Model X, and although there may be a greater emphasis on international deliveries, it's likely that your best bet for getting a 2017 or early 2018 delivery is if you reside in North America.

In addition, Tesla will likely deliver higher-priced versions of Model 3 before it begins delivery of base versions of the car. This is something to keep in mind as you

> **@evannex_com** **Order a Model 3 with lots of options. It's likely that your car will get delivery priority. #CarBling #Bigger$FasterDelivery**

configure your vehicle (Chapter 3). If you choose a Model 3 with a larger battery and lots of pricey options, it's likely that your car will come off the line before a naked base version of Model 3. This has been Tesla's early delivery approach with other cars in its product line, and it's reasonable to assume that it will continue.

Having said all of that, I'll provide you with a step-by-step approach for making an educated guess about when you might expect to receive your Model

> **@evannex_com** **Is there a way you can "guesstimate" when you'll get your car? Yes. But beware WAGs! #GuesstheDate**

3. To do this, you'll use the delivery ramp and production rate predictions I made earlier in this chapter, coupled with known Model 3 reservation history discussed in the last section.

**Step 1.** Use the following guidelines if you made your reservation for Model 3 on the very first day AND:

- If you were among the first 100 reservation holders in the door of any of the 92 Tesla stores in the United States, assume you're in the first 10,000 reservations.[45]

- If you made your reservation on the morning of March 31, 2016, assume you're among the first 30,000 on the list in the United States.

---

45. I'm assuming, possibly incorrectly, that Tesla will adjust the reservation numbers to reflect differences in time zones across the country.

- If you made your reservation later in the day of March 31, 2016, but before on-line reservations opened, assume you're in the first 40,000 on the list in the United States.

- If you made your reservation on-line before 6:00am on April 1, 2016, assume you're in the first 80,000 on the list in the United States.

**Step 2.** If you made your Model 3 reservation anytime on or after April 1, 2016, use the reservation history graph presented earlier and find the date on which you made your reservation.

- Project upward to find the approximate number of people in front of you on the list.

- To adjust for the fact that international reservations will be delivered later and that some people will cancel their reservations, use a number that represents about 60 percent of the vertical axis value on the graph.

**Step 3.** Go to Tables 1, 2, 3 or 4 and look at the "cumulative cars" column. Find the value that is just above the reservation number that you determined in either Step 1 or 2. Look across that row of the table to get a "guesstimate" of the year and quarter that you might expect delivery of your Model 3.

## A Few Delivery Scenarios[46]

**Scenario #1.** You got to the line at your local Tesla store two hours before opening on March 31, 2016. About 100 people were in front of you. Once the store opened, the line moved very quickly, and by 10:40 am your Model 3 reservation was recorded on a Tesla representative's tablet. From the criteria noted in Step 1 you can assume you're in the first 10,000 reservations in the U.S. Now, looking at Table 1, you'll see that delivery projections indicate that about 3,250 cars will be delivered by the end of 3Q17 and

46. I don't mean to belabor this, but please, please recognize that these are guesstimates only. The date you determine might be off by many months, depending on circumstances that cannot be foreseen at this time.

24,700 by the end of 4Q17. Because cars will be produced at an average rate of 1,650 per week during 4Q17, a likely delivery date will be late October or early November, 2017.

> **@evannex_com** **If you got on the list on day one, it's likely you'll get your Model 3 sometime in 2017 or early 2018. #GuesstheDate**

**Scenario # 2.** You signed up on-line after the Model 3 reveal on March 31, 2016. From the criteria noted in Step 1 you can assume you're in the first 80,000 reservations in the U.S. Now, looking at Table 2, you'll see that about 83,000 cars will have been delivered by the end of 2Q18. Your likely delivery date will be in late June, 2018.

**Scenario # 3.** You placed your reservation on April 6, 2016. Using the graph for Model 3 reservations, you estimate that there are about 300,000 people ahead of you. To adjust for international orders that will be delivered later and reservation cancellations, you take 60 percent of that total—180,000. Checking Table 2, you see that I project about 171,000 cars will be delivered by the end of 4Q18 and 226,000 cars will be delivered by the end of 1Q19. It's reasonable to assume that your car will be delivered in January, 2019.

Applying the same steps and the same reasoning, along with my projections of Model 3 production rate and reservation history, you can generate a guesstimate for when your Model 3 will be delivered.

> **@evannex_com** **You can wish all you like and jettison reality if you want, but building and delivering a revolutionary car takes time. Think 2018 or early 2019. #GuessTheDate #PatienceIsAVirtue #TeslaTime**

## Delivering the News

I did these projections to give you some feel for when your Model 3 might be delivered and to manage your expectations. As I mentioned at the beginning of this chapter, Tesla may surprise us all and ramp up deliveries much more rapidly than I project. Elon Musk argues that will happen. If it does, all Model 3 reservations on the list as of May, 2016, including those on the international list, might be satisfied by late 2018. But to be honest, I don't think that's likely.

**The Bad News.** As you can see from the speculative data presented in this chapter, the delivery ramp and projected production rates indicate that deliveries will take time. At first, it will be frustratingly slow, but Tesla does that for good reasons. Deliveries will accelerate, but given best guesses for production rate, it's possible that fewer than 172,000 Model 3s will be delivered by the end of 2018. Unless my estimates for the delivery ramp are way off (and they might be), anyone who got on the list after mid-April will probably have to wait until early 2019 before their Model 3 is delivered.

**The Good News.** If you're low on the reservation list, say, lower than 25,000, it's likely that your Model 3 will be delivered in late 2017. You'll be one of the few lucky owners that will be stopped in parking lots, asked hundreds of questions from adoring fans, and otherwise have bragging rights as owner of one of the coolest cars on the planet. If you went on the list in the first 5 or 6 days it was open, you have a good chance of getting your car in 2018.

Model 3 (Photo © Kyle Field, 2016, courtesy of Clean Technica)

It's fair to say that the wait will be worth it, but I've been there, and it can be frustrating. Just remember that patience is a virtue. To that end, perhaps it's best to quote[47] Tesla Motors CEO Elon Musk. He once said, "Patience is a virtue, and I'm learning patience. It's a tough lesson."

47. http://www.wired.com/2008/08/musk-qa/

# CHAPTER NINE
## THE COST OF OWNING MODEL 3

In a 2014 article at greentransportation.com. David Herron writes bluntly about EV economics:

> It's all well and good to buy an electric vehicle to save the planet, or because it's the latest cool thing, but what about your pocketbook?
>
> Unfortunately at the moment electric vehicles cost more to purchase than equivalent gasoline or diesel powered ones. Altruism goes only so far, and many people are unwilling to spend much more to purchase a different vehicle just because it is cleaner.
>
> You can argue that this is short-sighted because we all need to take strong action to avert various crises, but these people have a valid point about the economics of the situation.

That leads to a fundamental question. Is it possible to economically justify the purchase of an EV? And more importantly, is it possible to economically justify the purchase of a Model 3?

The answer to both questions is "yes," although a variety of factors influence the size of the economic benefit.

When considering these factors, you can also evaluate just how many (sometimes pricey) add-ons make sense for your Model 3.

**Cost**
**Will vary**

**Cost**
**Is different**

**Cost**
**Matters**

### BEV Economics

Many argue a BEV cost premium (often due to the expensive nature of lithium-ion batteries) can be offset by the long term cost savings associated with owning a BEV. But is the offset real?

That depends on the length of ownership—will you own the car for 3 years or 10. Obviously, the longer you own, the bigger any accumulated annual savings will be. It also depends on the cost of gasoline and electricity during the term of ownership—gas prices can fluctuate wildly and the cost of electricity varies significantly from state to state. If you decide to lease, any cost savings that are realized must be amortized across the term of the lease.

> @evannex_com **The decision to buy a Model 3 is emotional, even if the justification is numerical. #WantingModel3**

But if you're honest with yourself, you may have to admit that you signed up for a Tesla Model 3, not because you did a detailed economic analysis, but because you just plain wanted one. Your decision was emotional—and that's perfectly okay. The Model 3 is an awesome car, so it's very hard to factor emotion out of the buying decision.

It's been my experience that BEV buyers tend to be slightly more technical than the average car buyer and are somewhat more inclined to crunch the numbers in an effort to justify their 'buy' decision. But I'm not sure that really matters.

For many BEV buyers, including those who have indicated a desire for Model 3, a strong desire to see EVs happen—for any of a number of reasons—probably outweighs quantitative arguments.

Having said that, it's worth looking at the quantitative side briefly.

## Running the numbers

The first thing that you'll have to consider is this: what numbers do you look at and how do you generate them? It's a good idea to compare the ownership costs of a BEV against the ownership costs an equivalent ICE vehicle.

According to the American Automobile Association, the overall annual ownership costs for the average ICE vehicle are shown in the pie chart. Costs are predicated on 15,000 miles per year of travel.

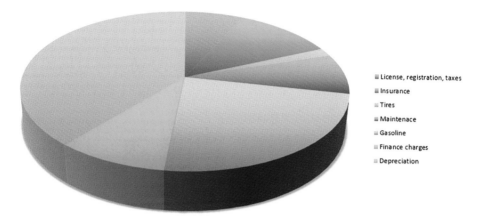

- License, registration, taxes
- Insurance
- Tires
- Maintenace
- Gasoline
- Finance charges
- Depreciation

Breakdown of annual ownership costs for an ICE vehicle

For an ICE vehicle, the cost of fuel (lighter blue slice) accounts for almost a quarter of the total yearly cost to own. Vehicle maintenance (purple slice) accounts for about 8 percent. These two categories represent potential cost savings when you trade your ICE vehicle for Model 3.

## The Real Cost of Model 3

To begin, it's important to understand the cost components that you'll need to evaluate the cost of ownership of Model 3.

**Overall cost of ownership = fuel costs + depreciation + maintenance costs + support costs**

where:

**Maintenance costs = cost of repairs + cost of consumables + cost of battery replacement**

**Support costs = Insurance + Financing costs + the cost of building a home charging infrastructure**

It's important to note that federal, and in some cases, state tax credits are available for certain classes of BEVs. These reduce the initial purchase price and help defray the so-called "EV premium" that currently exists. I'll talk about these later in this chapter.

**Fuel costs.** The cost for gas or diesel fuel accounts for almost 25 percent of yearly ownership costs for ICE cars. It's important to determine how much can be saved by getting your "fuel" from a wall socket in your garage as opposed to getting your fuel at a gas station.

Fueling Model 3 and Fueling ICE

First, you should project fuel costs for gasoline or diesel today and into the future and then do the same for electricity. Then, use fuel efficiency data (MPG and MPGe) for Model 3 and a similar ICE vehicle (i.e., similar in size and performance). Finally, use the number of miles per year you drive and the number of years of ownership or lease to estimate overall fuel cost and fuel cost savings for Model 3. A popular shortcut for determining your fuel savings is to visit: http://energy.gov/maps/egallon

**Depreciation.** It's far too early to assess the depreciation for Model 3, but it is fair to say that it's probably about the same as an ICE car in the same vehicle class. In fact, the resale value of Tesla automobiles is quite good when compared to similar ICE vehicles.

**Maintenance Costs.** The Institute for Automobile Economics (IFA) reports that, "electric vehicles partially compensate for high initial purchase prices by granting owners savings up to 35 percent in maintenance costs." This study was conducted in Europe for cars that traveled only 5000 miles per year, far below US averages. But it's fair to assert that additional miles traveled would increase, not decrease maintenance costs.

| Maintenance | ICE | BEV |
| --- | --- | --- |
| Oil change | 10 changes | 0 |
| Fluids | 1 change | 0 |
| Tires | 2 changes | 2 changes |
| Muffler | 1 change | 0 |
| Brakes | 1 change | 0 |
| Transmission | Service possible | none |
| Plugs | Service possible | none |

Maintenance requirements for ICE and BEV vehicles

The table illustrates the maintenance required for ICE vehicles and BEVs over 50,000 miles or about 5 years. Most of the typical maintenance expenses (e.g., oil changes) encountered for ICE vehicles simply disappear for BEVs. Also note that the relative inconvenience and time associated with auto maintenance visits are reduced considerably. It's very likely that your Model 3 will require only a yearly service visit, and that's it.

**Battery Replacement.** If you intend to own your Model 3 for many years, battery replacement cost is worth considering in an economic analysis, but it's not as ominous as some media hype indicates. BEV batteries can lose as much as 10% of their capacity at 50,000 miles and about 20% at 100,000 miles, assuming the typical number of charging cycles associated with that level of mileage. But a mildly degraded battery still works fine. You get less range, but otherwise, your car keeps operating with no ill effects.

> @evannex_com **Any battery will degrade with time, just like an ICE will degrade with time.**

It's likely that by the time you might have to replace your battery, (say at about 150,000 to 200,000 miles, battery costs will likely be in the $100 per kWh range, meaning that a ~60kWh battery might cost about $6,000 to replace. That's about the same cost as a new ICE engine and transmission, which might need to be replaced in the same timeframe as a BEV battery replacement. Also, keep in mind that some observers have suggested that Model 3 will have a minimum eight year battery warranty based on Tesla's current warranty policies.

**Cost of a PCI.** We discussed many of the considerations for building a personal charging infrastructure (PCI) in Chapter 5. The overall cost varies with the complexity of the installation, whether or not an EVSE is required (as yet unknown for Model 3) and other factors associated with your residential setting. At the low end, a PCI can cost as little as $400 to $500 to install. At the high end (where you foot the bill for an apartment parking installation), it can cost thousands of dollars.

**Tax Credit.** There is a $7,500 federal tax credit available for buyers of zero-emission EVs. In some cases, specific states also offer tax credits that vary from $0 to $6,000 (not to mention some nice perks like free access to car pool lanes and special parking places at public facilities). But there's a catch.

Special parking for low emission vehicles

Under the current IRS regulations, the federal tax credit reduces to zero once a specific manufacturer sells more than 200,000 zero-emission vehicles. Once the 200,000-car threshold is reached, the tax credit reduces to $3,750 for the next six months as additional EVs are sold, and $1,875 for the following six months. It then phases out altogether.

Given current sales of Model S and Model X, it's likely that Tesla will reach the 200,000-car threshold at the end of 2017, taking projected (Chapter 8) deliveries of Model 3 into account. It remains to be seen how this all unfolds, but I wouldn't count on the $7,500 federal tax credit as a "sure thing" for Model 3 deliveries in 2018.

> **@evannex_com If you're low on the reservation list, you'll probably get a tax credit, but it will not be $7,500. #FedsWillHelp**

That said, if production ramps as rapidly as I have predicted, it may be that a fairly large number of Model 3 owners will receive the $3,750 credit during the six months following the threshold being met, and an even larger number of owners would get the smaller $1,875 credit over the following six months. Using my projections from Chapter 8 (Tables 2 and 3), it's possible that 25,000 to 40,000 Model 3 owners in the United States could get the full $7,500 credit, and another 150,000 could receive either a $3,750 credit or the smaller $1,875 credit. After that—no tax credit will be available unless the legislation is renewed and modified.

# CHAPTER TEN
## THE GIGAFACTORY

It's reasonable to ask a fundamental question about the cost of BEVs in general and Model 3 in particular. Because BEVs have significantly fewer parts than conventional ICE vehicles, why do they typically cost more, not less?

The reason is the cost of the battery. Today, battery costs are proprietary to most automobile manufacturers including Tesla. However, some insights were gleaned when Electrek[48] reported that Jon Bereisa, CEO of Auto Lectrification and former chief engineer of the Chevy Volt program, said "Tesla's current battery pack cost (cells, casing, cooling and entire pack) is at $260/kWh, while GM's is at $215/kWh." However, Tesla's Vice-President of Investor Relations, Jeff Evanson refuted Bereisa and "stated that Tesla's battery pack cost is already below $190/kWh."

**Big**
**Plans**
**Big**
**Savings**
**Big**
**Factory**

Assuming Tesla makes progress leading up to Model 3 launch and achieves battery costs in the $100 - $150 per kWh range, this would prove to be a substantial reduction in cost. A ~60 kWh battery for Model 3, built under that battery cost model, would add about $6,000 to $9,000 to the cost of the vehicle. Tesla's goal is to reduce battery costs substantially—thereby keeping Model 3 costs under control and setting the stage for an even more inexpensive "fourth generation" Tesla vehicle at some future date.[49]

48. Lambert, F., ""Tesla confirms that base Model 3 will have less than 60 kWh battery pack option ...", electrek, April 26, 2016, available at: http://electrek.co/2016/04/26/tesla-model-3-battery-pack-cost-kwh/

Artist's rendering of the Gigafactory while under construction

At the core of Tesla's low cost battery strategy lies the "Gigafactory" —an enormous industrial facility dedicated to the manufacture of batteries. Located on "Electric Avenue" in Sparks, NV (outside of Reno) and connected by rail to Tesla's factory in Freemont, CA, the Gigafactory has been designed to run on solar energy from a multi-acre solar array on its roof.

Lauren Sommer[50] describes the facility:

> Tesla expects the factory, created in partnership with Panasonic, to double the world's capacity for lithium-ion battery production, eventually making 35 gigawatt-hours of energy storage annually. That would supply 500,000 of its electric cars, a significant leap over what the company is producing now. Tesla executives estimate that when fully operational, economies of scale will drive the cost of batteries down by 30 percent or more.

The Gigafactory is partially complete and operational and, according to Tesla, will be brought on-line in stages as various sections of the factory are completed. One of the operational sections of the factory currently produces the Tesla *Powerwall*—a 4 foot x 3 foot flat storage battery that is used to store 7 kWh of energy for residential use. In essence, a homeowner could charge the battery by day (from the grid or from a solar array on the roof of

**@evannex_com The Gigafactory is one of the largest manufacturing buildings in the United States. #gigafactory**

49. Pressman, M, "Elon Musk: Tesla will follow up the Model 3 with a Fourth Generation, Lower Priced Electric Vehicle, April 23, 2016, available at: http://evannex.com/blogs/news/116325573-elon-musk-tesla-will-follow-up-the-model-3-with-a-fourth-generation-lower-priced-electric-vehicle

the house) and then use the energy stored in the Powerwall when a regular power source is unavailable. The Powerwall would make solar usage practical on a 24-hour basis and might obviate the need for a home generator for short-term power outages.

The industrial-strength version of Powerwall is a refrigerator-sized *Powerpack*, used by commercial customers and utilities to store power for use during peak demand periods.

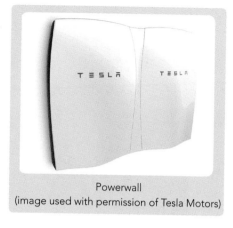

Powerwall
(image used with permission of Tesla Motors)

But let's get back to Model 3. The Gigafactory will undoubtedly help Tesla achieve it's base model price point, but it could also allow Tesla to offer battery upgrades for Model 3 (e.g., a larger battery for a performance version of the car) at a reasonable price. This might allow Tesla to offer greater range and performance for a price that makes economic sense for a larger subset of future Model 3 owners.

Tesla Powerpack
(image used with permission of Tesla Motors)

50. Sommer, L., "Inside Tesla's Mysterious Desert Battery factory," KQED Science, April 15, 2016, avialable at: http://ww2.kqed.org/science/2016/04/15/inside-teslas-mysterious-desert-battery-factory/

# CHAPTER ELEVEN
## A 21ST CENTURY CAR FOR EVERYONE

As I stood in front of the stage at Tesla design center as Elon Musk introduced the Model 3, the excitement in the room was akin to what you would experience at a major sporting event or rock concert. You could feel it. But all the people in the room were Tesla fans, so it was a little difficult to determine whether Model 3 would resonate with those in the outside world. Sure, the long lines at Tesla stores provided some outside evidence, but what were the initial preorder numbers?

After Musk's presentation, two Model 3s were driven off-stage to be used for test rides. Some in the crowd went outside to watch the preparations, to talk with Tesla reps, to visit with one another, to give interviews with the media, to drink and eat. But some of us stayed inside to take photos of the beautiful red Model 3 that remained on stage.

Suddenly, an enormous digital counter was projected onto the backdrop of the stage. Like a digital counter measuring a rapidly changing phenomenon, the lower digits rotated quickly, 122,353 ... 122,468 ... a few minutes later ... 123,233 ... The digital counter was tracking incoming online reservations for Model 3, and

**Think**
**New car**
**Think**
**New future**
**Think**
**Model 3**

it was moving fast, very fast. It became instantly apparent that the Model 3 was a home run, that media projections of 25,000 or 50,000 sign-ups in the first month were a joke, and that with this car, Tesla Motors would jolt the automotive world in a way that hadn't been done in a century. Model 3 is different, but at the end of the day, it's still just a car. You'll drive (or be driven autonomously) to work, visit friends, go to events, and take long trips, just the way you always have.

In this book, I've tried to get you ready for Model 3 by introducing some of the core concepts that you'll need to understand, some of the Model 3 features you'll undoubtedly encounter as you configure your car, some of the issues associated with range, charging, and autonomous driving,

The Tesla Model 3 (Photo © Kyle Field, 2016, courtesy of Clean Technica)

and finally, provide you with some indication of when you might realistically expect to get your Model 3. In all, I've tried to prepare you for a car that just might change things dramatically in the automotive world.

Model 3 is a 21st century car for almost everyone. It delivers style, technology, and performance in a car that is simply better—for the planet, for the driver, for the industry. It will change things … and that's what Tesla Motors is all about.

# INDEX